Entering Fire

ENTERING FIRE

Rikki Ducornet

City Lights Books
San Francisco

Library of Congress Cataloging-in-Publication Data
Ducornet, Rikki, 1943–
    Entering Fire.
    Reprint. Originally published: England: Chatto & Windus, Ltd., 1986
    I. Title.
PS3554.U279E5   1987   813'.54   87-15830
ISBN 0-87286-207-0   (pbk.)

CITY LIGHTS BOOKS are edited by Lawrence Ferlinghetti
& Nancy J. Peters and published at the City Lights Bookstore,
261 Columbus Avenue, San Francisco CA 94133.

For Jean-Yves and Mary-Jane

ACKNOWLEDGEMENTS

I wish to thank orchidologists Messieurs Vacherot and Lecoufle and Monsieur Pierre Fradin for their passionate and precise descriptions of the cloning process; Christian Laucou for trusting me with his rare copies of Ananké's *Hel!*; Pierre Sabourin for books and for orchids; my father for giving me the coveted *History Of Coca* by Mortimer; Wendy for the *Manuel d'exercices de style*, 1858 (the book which provided for Virginie's conversation); and above all Guy, as ever.

'The incomparable clavicord of Marie Antoinette stood like a trophy in the middle of the room. It was heartbreaking to see it in the house of Jews.' *Les Rothschild*, Anonymous, 1894

'There's always a little Jew squatting in the corner, jeering and touching himself.' *Les Beaux Draps*, L.-F. Céline, 1941

'BA-HEL . . . BAL . . . BEL . . . BALTIQUE, ALBANY, BÔ (PO), Lybie etc.' *Hel! Visions préhistoriques*, Ananké, 1928

'When afraid, the Jew is really very charming.' *Testament d'un antisémite*, Eduard Drumont, 1881

'May I have the floor?' Senator McCarthy, Army McCarthy Hearings, 1954

'You understand . . . It's Fairyland.' *Féerie pour une autre fois*, L.-F. Céline, 1941

CHAPTER ONE

EMERGENCIES OF THE IMAGINATION

Septimus de Bergerac

P'pa, although a de Bergerac, a Frenchman and married to my mother, had a Chinese concubine. He brought her back from a voyage to Peking in the spring of 1881. M'man took one look at the woman's tiny, cloven hooves and swollen belly and before fainting shouted, 'Kremlin and Vatican!', the only curse she knew. The infidel's name was Dust.

M'man, a valiant Frenchwoman and an honour to her race, accepted the situation. To question P'pa's decisions was beyond her wildest imaginings. Indeed, M'man was an exemplarily virtuous woman and had no imagination.

A shadow, more echo than flesh, Dust kept to her room. It stank of the skeletons of sea-moths she kept in a basket beneath her bed. She broke off pieces of this refuse for steeping, and drank the noxious broth.

Pauvre Maman! She had been sired by a Grenier de Fourtou, a founding member of the Anti-Semitic League of France. A weaker woman, a woman less devoted to loyalty and peace, would have gone insane. Sharing one's roof with a Chinawoman is quite as bad as sharing it with a Rothschild. At death's door she confided to me that before P'pa had left for China to study kiwis (or was it lychees?) they had shared but seven chaste nights. And that, having conceived me upon his return, she never slept with him again. M'man's name was Virginie: *Virgo! Vis! Virtu!*

Dust was given the maid's quarters and the maid removed to the attic where she grew despondent. She was replaced by a sallow, ill-tempered wench whose skin and soul were thicker.

Mademoiselle Parfait did not mind draughts. And when Dust went insane (hers is a weak race, inbred since the times of *tohubohu* stewing, so to speak, in its own primal juices) P'pa tumbled with that dour sow up in her pigsty. Often I would hide beneath the stairs and listen to their heavy breathing. Half frozen with cold and loathing, I would slither back to my bed and like a little lizard curled within a crack, weep and pray for M'man.

The first week Dust spent rolled up in a curtain. She explained as best she could to P'pa that she wanted First Wife to know that she, Dust, was less than an insect, a species of larva.

As her feet were the size and shape of the tiny paper boats Mademoiselle Parfait set afloat in my bath, Dust could walk only with the help of two ebony canes. The minutes of my young life were counted by their barbaric drumming on the ceiling overhead. And as I sit on the floor looking at the forbidden photographs that P'pa has brought back from his travels, their thump, thump hammers each image into the tender surface of my mind. The heavy, cerise volume, Mademoiselle Parfait teases, is bound in human skin, and the raised rosebud centred on the cover in a wreath of leaves is a human nipple. She continues: 'Your P'pa has visited many strange and savage lands where the livers of bull elephants and the shrunken heads of little boys are mere currency, like coins.'

The photographs in P'pa's album are hideous and they are True. That they are True cannot be doubted. Perhaps I owe my astonishing precocity to them – without false modesty, I have always been something of a genius. (I am, by the way, the author of *The Rothschild Plot* – a work which has had undeniable impact upon contemporary French History.)

Back to P'pa's album. I turn the thick pages, the colour of

bone, encrusted with the monstrous visions of naked savages and savage punishments. The cannibals of Dahomy stand in the city of Ouida (known to the ancients as Juda – these creatures are descended from one of the lost tribes of Israel) hugging sacks of human meat, like medieval Jews on their way to market. There are photographs of the truncated crooks of Tonkin and of child whores hanging from their feet in the pleasure palaces of Peking, of nude New Caledonians with rags tied to their foreskins. Dust's thump, thump, thump stabs my ribs like the finger of a cannibal rabbi. Or is it the merciless staff of Father Time I hear ticking and tocking?

In the fall of 1881, the Chinese trollop gave P'pa a son; or rather, the foul fermentations and stinking incubations of an infamous heredity produced my half-brother who, despite the fact that his mother was no larger than a doll, and that my father was himself a small man, even for a Frenchman, grew to be unusually tall and broad and who, from infancy, I despised. He was fifteen when Dust died of influenza and was reduced by fire to a thimbleful of oily ashes. He became so wild that the following year while P'pa was in the Amazon chewing coca, M'man sent him from the house. Two years later he was arrested in Le Havre for the murder of Lady Aurora, the English prostitute. She had been beaten to death with a blunt instrument, perhaps a cane. The descriptions of the affair were as numerous as the newspapers reporting it. Misogynist I have often thought of this violent murder with satisfaction as if I had committed it myself. Yes, I envy my enormous, slant-eyed brother for having had the audacity and the imagination to perpetrate the mad act that I have not dared commit except by proxy or in fantasies imposed upon public women – preferably yellow, Arab or Semite, whose smell of cheap soap and powder, whose every mole, scar and hair I despise as passionately as I crave. In the act I have murdered thousands. It is fortunate for men like myself that for money there are many who will allow themselves to be beaten black and blue with a hairbrush. Yet I have on occasion been slapped and once even spat at by an animal who, despite base blood and even baser calling, had not yet sold her pride. These few, very few, angry and vain beasts are the only members of the sex (except, *évidemment*, M'man) for whom I have felt, mingled with loathing, an emotion that might possibly begin to approach what some men call admiration. I am thinking in particular of a Jewess, her red hair framing her face like a hoop of fire, who dared kick me in the chest with a small, satin-slippered foot. That instant of pain and shock, as the sharp heel thumped against my startled heart, was an instant – the only instant – that I believe I might have felt tenderness.

Yet, I have never admired anyone (apart from M'man) except – and isn't it odd, for when I think of him even now I lose sleep – that hated half-brother whom M'man neglected to have baptized and to whom Dust gave the name Chên-Yen: True Man.

Mine is a life punctuated by an incessant thump, thump. And now that I've a cane myself – having lost the use of a leg to syphilis (God damn the gypsy whores and their hook-nosed Semite pimps!) – it amuses me no end, I assure you, to jab and stab along my own chosen paths.

I was born white and male in my mother's bed, in the same bed in which I had been conceived and, thank Heaven, not P'pa's ancestral bed: a nest of heretics, felons and fools. Like all mortals damned with life, I stumbled out a bloody mess and squalling. The first sounds I heard were the sounds of M'man panting for air, and Dust feverishly scrambling over-head. Her quarters were directly above M'man's bedroom;

the two women could not have known each other more intimately had they been twins.

True Man was born shortly after (he held onto the foetal state for fifteen months like a giraffe) and, although he was born later, he was from the start, bigger. At one year he was walking (he learned holding on to his mother's canes), when I was forever sitting in M'man's lap. True Man was the first to talk. By the time he was twelve months' old, he could carry on a conversation with his mother in Chinese and with Mademoiselle Parfait in French. Tongue-tied at three I could barely stutter, but by then I could walk. P'pa had an obvious preference for his Mongol cub who strutted proudly in pants at a time when I was still dragging my diapers.

We were put together in the freshly painted nursery. There Dust spent the odd hours of the day and M'man the even (but for meals when we were fed by the dour Mademoiselle Parfait). M'man read us the fairytales of Perrault from a dainty, faded blue book which had been her own, and Dust, her pygmy shoes brushing my cheek, True Man hanging from her neck, recited the revulsive inventions of her homeland in a baffling jabber. These True Man translated, much to my humiliation. I should not have listened – they might well have infected my brain: feudal tales of insatiable Mongol murderers; of embalmed Emperors and rivers of mercury; of an imperial cadaver that stank so shockingly it was bedded down in a half ton of salt fish.

We were never alone. Mademoiselle took us out for tonic walks and severely chaperoned our games. I have a memory that nags like a rotten tooth. I had been locked in the cellar for naughtiness. True Man came home from a pony ride in the Jardin du Mail, smelling of hay, pistachio ice-cream dribbled all over his chin. It was the first time I ever bit anyone.

I never did understand Dust. I was 'First Wife's Son', and

'Older Son'; she bowed reverently before me – even when I was a toddler – and punished me whenever she had the chance. In turn, M'man punished True Man. Dust was a pincher, an ear-twister and a penis-tweaker; M'man favoured dark corners, the cellar and cold baths. Their punishments were maddening and incessant. True Man once said that our childhood lasted one thousand years. And, if I was green with envy, he was yellow with bile.

Like the Jews, the Chinese have the ways of Bedouins. Before she expired of the influenza that made off with eighty people in the winter of 1896, Dust went mad. Her madness seized her one summer's day as she sat in her dank room gazing out of the open window. The air was so still and heavy, it did nothing to dissipate the nauseous odours of mummification that hovered about her like a fog. Dust pointed to M'man's favourite tree – a lime – and shrieked that it was plotting against her life. And if, when excited, republicans wave their flags, freemasons their ignominious bric-à-brac and Jews their stocks and bonds, Dust, dwarfed in her midnight blue longevity garment, her face powdered deathly white, waved her canes: 'Thlashing devils!' She scribbled her nightmares on triangles of red paper and gave them to True Man to burn; she attempted to transfer her fears to a cricket she kept in a comb-box and her spiritual agony to a spider that lived over the door. The simplest tasks – mending a garment, plucking her eyebrows, washing her crippled feet – exposed her to danger. She tickled her nostrils with a feather and sneezed, expulsing malignant influences. She took to sleeping beneath her bed, her longevity robe stained and clotted with filth, clutching to her heart a silk purse which contained the Devil knows what. And when she could sleep no more, she spent the long nights fumbling in the dark after headless chickens, the spirits of snakes and goblins, swatting at scorpions and jinn. Again she screamed. Mademoiselle Parfait did not see the warlocks clinging to the ceiling like flies, even when one hit her with a turd. But she agreed to bring opium from the pharmacy. Dust grew quiet and stopped eating. M'man prayed to the Virgin Mary. And one night Dust saw a spirit wearing a yellow apron and chewing betel. She recognized the royal executioner. 'The Guilty Head!' she raved. 'The Guilty Head is cut!' She saw True Man's neck marked with the executioner's red spittle. True Man had not yet committed his crime, yet somehow Dust knew all about it. Ravaged by fever, within a week she was dead. M'man took the crushed-leather missal, decorated with a cross of diamond powder, which had belonged to P'pa's mother, and gave it to the priest to be burned along with the body. Privately she jubilated. Because Dust was Chinese, she could not be buried in the cemetery. Mademoiselle Parfait spilled the ashes – in which the diamond powder could be seen shining – into the Loire. To this day I cannot eat river fish; nor can I hear the word 'yellow' without succumbing to a fit of evil temper. Indeed I cannot say 'Chinese' without biting my tongue.

And now I will make a confession: I have despised my father from the instant I understood the impossible situation he had imposed upon M'man. And I fantasize that I was not fathered by the greasy, barrel-chested bigamist, but, rather, by Monsieur Kindergarten the masseur, although this is ridiculous. I look nothing like Monsieur Kindergarten and have inherited everything in cruel caricature from P'pa: the bulbous nose like a Dutchman's, and puffy eyes, the cheeks like putty, the coarse, untameable hair and so on. Whereas Monsieur Kindergarten is all Elegance: svelte, sure-footed and as muscular as Atlas. Yet I persist in my little fairytale that the masseur is my papa, and I have learned to mimic that springy gait, that genial buoyancy, that impressive something or other which smacks of Health and Dependability.

Monsieur Kindergarten was an important feature in my young life, more for what he evoked than for what he was. His was a shadowy figure, and swiftly passing. Always discreet and always on time, he slipped into M'man's chamber each afternoon at four o'clock. I knew she lay upon her bed like a bride or a corpse, clothed only in a sheet and expectancy.

I like to think that once, as M'man lay palpitating beneath his fingers, Monsieur Kindergarten had slipped judiciously in; that his silent torrent had rushed her grotto like a storm, that the blind comet breaching the moon of M'man's molten ovum *was to become me*. But all this is, *hélas*, impossible. For when Monsieur Kindergarten came into my life, I was already seven years old, and the inexorable pattern of my birth and life set down forever. And if I have learned to imitate the man's walk and manner, his fingers still elude me – fingers as muscular as a bull's neck and capable of scaling a perpendicular mountain of ice. I hasten to add that, although my fingers are as weak as husked clams, *I am as white as he*. My skin like putty, my bulbous nose and barrel chest – ugly as they are – are *white*.

1888 is the year Monsieur Kindergarten enters our lives and the year P'pa leaves for South America. When she learns of his decision, Dust slams her forehead against his boots – a shocking sight. M'man passes out, spilling the potted plants, and Mademoiselle Parfait runs for salts. I should explain that P'pa's wanderlust frittered away M'man's dowry and his own inheritance – the fortune accumulated by his grandfather in the salt mines of French Morocco. M'man's head hot in my lap, my hatred egging me on, I ask: Why? The cad's pretentious answer: 'A man must prove himself worthy of Paradise.'

That night he came into the nursery and attempted to justify

16

himself. True Man sat as if seduced or hypnotized; perhaps he was merely confused. I listened with loathing to fables of spiders the size of cauliflowers and lily pads the size of parlours and knew P'pa was mad.

'The Equator,' he lied, 'is a wall of solid gold bricks. I am on my way to Eden.'

Eden! P'pa left us for a sewer the size of a planet. A jungle where everything, even shit, shines in the dark. Just dreaming of it had robbed him of his precarious senses. He raved on, attempting to turn our heads with a sack full of mystical garbage. Thank God I was a born sceptic and sniggered at his lunatic fancies . . . He suggested that the world would one day be a gigantic eye – like the eye of a fly – covered from pole to pole with the junk lenses and trick mirrors of astronomy. He pretended that the Universe is a web floating on a breeze, the galaxies and nebulae but dew sparkling in its filaments.

P'pa gone, Dust sucked on knobs of desiccated sea-urchin, M'man wept and I – when I was not scuffling with True Man (that year I kicked him so severely in the head he almost died) – attempted to imagine that Hell-hole which had become P'pa's home. I traced his entire itinerary on the map and in my mind's eye, Argentina, soaked with the seed of gauchos, and scattered with the bleached bones of beef, is orange; Ecuador, despite its natives' sanguinary inclinations and the torrid heat, is a cool, mint green, and Brazil, thanks to the map-maker's incongruous imagination, is the colour of a virgin's bedroom: pale pink.

Sometime during the first year of his absence, I went into his library and burned the atlas, burned the thick and weighty volumes by the Bavarian naturalists Spix, Martius and Pohl, and burned his cherished Darwin. How I hate that monkey-business!

Ma pauvre Maman! The triumph of the Zionists, the horse-faced English, the communists and the American gum-poppers in 1944 was what stopped her long suffering heart. She was eighty-four. After her death I went through her journals, all written in her careful schoolgirl's hand, and came upon this beautiful piece which both expresses the nobility of her heart and explains, in part, the mystery of her hateful relationship with that hoodlum adventurer, my father.

'. . . The river flows on to the sea and no human power can turn it from its course. So it is with Time. The Lord God alone can stop its swift Progress. Yet, how I enjoy Old Age having survived Youth! A calm retirement is the Lord's most cherished gift. The Hero deserves Glory and the Old Respect.

Virtue, like a violet, brings quiet joy to those who see and smell her. So do I live and modestly with my son, doing my duty without Vanity. Septimus loves me unreservedly. The Afflicted deserve Consolation.

Even now the memory of my husband Lamprias is a thorn in my side that gathers no moss. It seems he was Fated to Torment me. The Unfortunate Lament their Fate.

As a girl I went to Convent School in Arles where I learned how to prepare a menu, inform, in convincing tones, a maid of her duties; to write a letter to an Older Woman and to an Elderly Man; to remove gloves and to wear a hat; to walk across a room and to buy lace; and the names of those few authors I could read with surety. I learned to enunciate in perfect English:

A starving man needs food.
A shoemaker needs leather.

I learned how to decorate a drawing room. Rooms need to be swept, it comes to me now, I also put to memory.

I knew all these things. Yet I was innocent and upon my Wedding Night I discovered that all that shines is not gold. Setting my eyes upon those immense and terrifying particulars that, until then, my husband had kept tucked away and hidden from the Light of Day, I fainted. The Virtuous have no eyes for Sin. And when I dared look, *hélas*, those Evil Goods were still in evidence. My husband made next to suckle me. I had married a man of Perverted Temperament! He attempted all that endless week to convince me that those foul objects were made by God for my pleasure – a blasphemy and an absurdity I refused to recognize for Truth. When I returned home, my dear mother explained that those lurid things were common to all men and the very gears which set the wheels of procreation in motion. The ultimate Insanity! I still cannot believe that this was His intention in the First Place, but an Aberration of a later epoque when the Devil had taken command of the Material World. However. Had Mother explained all this earlier, I might have managed to see something of Padirac.

A song, popular at the time, comes back to me now: 'A Daughter's Lament To Her Father Upon Being Married'. It was a song we girls at the Convent School sang as we sat together on our beds in our plain madapolam shifts:

> Tell me dear Papa what pleasure you find
> To have made me leave my virtue behind.
> Behind!
> Behind!
> My virtue behind!'

When on Christmas Eve, 1891 — his skin so tanned it had no recognizable colour but could only be described as fulvous — P'pa walked in the front door, he brought fever and the germs of an insane idea. That night at dinner he sent M'man running from the table in tears. I remember exactly what he said:

'In the Amazon, every fish is the spirit of a penis in search of an orchid. And every orchid is the spirit of a woman's vagina.'

CHAPTER TWO

ENTERING FIRE

Lamprias de Bergerac

I have always loved women, even my wife Virginie, who was frigid and a bigot to boot. This love of women has been inseparable from a burning desire to know. The Eternal Feminine throbs at the heart of Mystery.

I have loved Evangelista, a coffee-coloured giantess, who chewed sweet coca and who wore silk garters. I loved my Chinese concubine who, before she went mad, nibbled my balls as if they were lychees and kept my tail standing on end and barking for hours. In Rio an acrobatic blonde fed me curry with a spoon held between her toes. My first love, the stunning Marta Strada (whom Septimus my ignoble son was to sell to the Gestapo for kindling) I ravished in a French forest fragrant with morels. We were both sixteen. But, of all the women I have loved, my Heart of Hearts is the woman I found squatting by a low fire, gnawing on a grilled iguana: my snake of coral, my coca nymph, my tropical rain forest – *Cûcla*.

Distracted as I am by her memory, I am getting ahead of myself. My mind, tracked by forgetfulness, is like a child's kaleidoscope. And when I look back, time is no longer linear, but like an agitated cylinder filled with mirrors and bits of coloured glass. My memories spill and tumble and glimmer together – Marta Strada, Evangelista, Rosada the vampire who sucked the blood of ten thousand men, Tarantula Jane and the Blue Man – but it seems that most of the shining is Cûcla, my child-bride, my fragrant orchid. She winks in the brightest bits of glass, those I would reach for first, like the marbles little boys lust after. The prize tiger-eyes.

I'll start with Rio and then travel on. Now, as then, Rio can't keep me long, even though it was very beautiful, gilded by night with gas lights and shaded by day with blueblossomed jacaranda trees. It was here that I met the blonde with the toes – at the Copacabana Palace. Spanking new, with doormen like freshly painted figures of lead, brass orchestras, and Indian maids standing silently in starched linen, like duskydark blossoms seized in snow. Each one was sweeter than the next, sadder than the next. They missed the jungles, the swift reptile-infested waters and air like a thin ocean. Sirens of evening, they missed the Amazon Aquarium and they died, you know, like flies. When I left the Copacabana for the Forest of Fire, they said I'd never find it – that it had been swallowed up by Vampira. They meant the railroad, of course; the snake Cûcla called Greed.

I moved on. Left Rio's quiet backyards, perfumed with English roses and shaded by palms, a shade punctuated by the staccato of parrotchatter and the syncopated passage of lizards; left the boulevards, the gentlemen from Bristol, dressed in tails, who nonchalantly sipped iced *maté* after buggering little, lost Indios in the park behind the silent statuary. I tipped my new leather hat to the proud, new theatre – part temple, part saloon – where the world's handsomest women came to show off their soft arms and throats to the most elegant and the most enthusiastic public in the world.

Never in my life had I seen as many shoe-stores as there were in Rio – everyone wore fancy, leather shoes, except for the Indians who went barefoot – nor as many dentists. The rich food, no doubt, the famous Gremaldi Ices and iced drinks spiked with *cachaça*, the exotic candied fruits . . . Etched into my brain are visions of young, green Spanish girls sipping sherbet and preening like grebes on balconies, bouncy French whores nibbling pineapple and dealing out cards, English lasses floating past on imported bicycles and everywhere a European bustle of full skirts. Beneath the tropical sun the women sweated like mares – the odour of their overheated flesh was everywhere – their breasts pressed beneath the lace of their bodices like flowers in a book of verse. And now suddenly I remember the laundresses hanging out the city's wash to dry in the blazing sun. And camisoles and shifts and bloomers and petticoats. There were men in Rio, too, but I took little notice of them – coachmen and melon-hatted Englishmen, traders in cheese and tea, eager manufacturers of shoes and felt hats and glass and optical instruments; importers of telephones, layers of water pipes, exporters of rubber and rare wood; jittery monarchists, embittered sugar barons, vociferous republicans . . . the women, bless them, were too busy in their beds and baths to bother with commerce and politics.

The slaves had just been emancipated – it was a festive and anarchic time in Rio and a time of wild financial speculation. I might have been tempted to stay. But I hungered for the Forest of Fire. Cûcla was there, crouching in the shadows and waiting. Cûcla with her little laugh like bells, her little breasts like shells. Already she was tugging at my wand and the burntsugar smell of orchids was in the air, everywhere.

Until I had seen the forest, I thought the world was absurd because imperfect. But the forest, raw as it is and cruel, *fits*. It fits the way a man fits a woman; it fits that well and feels that good. There, like a boy in the bed of an ogress, a man must be fearless or die. God's fist it is. And God's eye.

From Rio I take a steamer, the *Cabocla Queen*, to Belem at the mouth of the Rio Para. We carry whisky and a load of Chinese furniture. I introduce myself to two lady adventurers – Uma and Förtjusande, both Swedes with gold teeth – who have brought along their brass beds. Belem is so hot everything has slowed down but for the vermin, which is fast. If a man doesn't keep on his toes, the ants will make off with his balls before he has a chance to blink. Belem is baroque, gorgeous, ordered, elegant. It also has its shanties, havens for the *gringos*, the railroad bums, the miserable sonsofwhores who have run away from Vampira. They crowd Belem's waterside bars, obsessed and angry and often dying. Beside the caged *chichocos* (the smallest monkeys in the world, the alchemist's homunculus with hair), garlands of shrunken heads, scalps and the skins of anacondas, they tell their stories. The railroad is a slaughter-house. Senhor Rosada of Valparáiso wants an iron road to take his rubber from the backlands directly to the Atlantic Coast. He shoots his men for drinking water. Shoots them for buggery. Shoots them for lying down sick. Shoots them for the hell of it. And the men, Chinese, Italian, Hindu, African live on mouldy hardtack, molasses and whisky, and they tear each other apart. And he whom beri-beri, yellow fever, dysentery or bullets do not kill, the exasperated Indians get with darts.

Sooner or later, most of the men go stark raving mad. Senhor Rosada shoots his own son for impertinence – he's a driven man, with the Devil nipping at his arse, a freewheeling tycoon who in his youth had made a fortune in dyewood and diamonds. Now that South African diamonds and aniline dyes have kicked a whopping hole in the market, he's sunk his money into Vampira and rubber. I discover that my steamer and its cargo belong to his company.

Meanwhile the Indians, their skin gleaming beneath caesalpinia dye the colour of red coals, are dreaming. They know

Vampira is monstrous, that she will dribble pus all over their land. Her ribs, say the dreams, are made of the bones of Indians. And the *gringos*, stinking of bad whisky, say she'll miscarry, that Rosada, for all his damned stubbornness and bloody money, will fail. And they will be proved right. Vampira will abort pestilence and the suppurating corpses of countless men. Like the elusive Emerald River, Vampira is just another lethal mirage.

I take leave of my new Swedish friends who stay on in Belem to quench the *gringos*' terminal fevers and collect what cash they can, and continue up the Amazon to São José. The voyage is peaceful, until we come to Óbidos, where the river narrows and the waters dance. As I look out to the harbour, the sky thickens with tiny, blue butterflies.

Just before we reach São José, we enter the confluence of the Amazon and the Rio Negro, where black and yellow waters flow side by side without mingling. My heart is singing and I am shaking with laughter – absolute joy! We dock at noon. Some sleazy characters unload the Chinese furniture. It is all for that devil Rosada.

Six hundred kilometres from the sea, São José is a sumptuous city of palaces, bordellos and saloons, her streets scorching with fancy whores and the hot glances of the Rubber Baron's spoiled and high-strung daughters. Everything is for sale: curare, guns and magic roots, songs and aphrodisiacs and, above all, land. Speculators snap up tracks of forest and start up a company. They sell weevilled rice, poor equipment and Rio de Janeiro gin to desperate men who will not live to cancel their debt but will die hallucinating after the rubber which grows scattered. These days Brazil's veins of silver and gold have been bled to a thin trickle, but the trees are pissing sap and some clever fellow is manufacturing the pneumatic tyre. Senhor Rosada's eyes are shining – the government is minting money as if it were made of sugar and he's received a letter from an enterprising young man named Henry Ford.

Here, in São José, I meet Evangelista. This black-eyed, violet-tongued *cafuso* is a volcanic fusion of Ivory Coast and Xvante, a powerhouse with a voice like the horn of an Easter Islander and an Easter Island type of monumentality. She lords it over everyone, even the newly liberated black colossuses who have left the *fazendas* for São José, the malarial jungle and the elusive riches Rosada's men have promised them.

'Damn fools!' she scolds the men who have signed away their new found freedom. 'That bitch rubber's blind man's bluff. Murder. Eat you up.'

Evangelista is already legendary. In the later days of dye-wood and diamonds, she cost Rosada a fortune. Driven mad by the company whisky, and inspired by Evangelista's cry for Justice, the men blew a company steamer sky-high. She is still alive only because Rosada believes that his diamonds were smuggled to her before a hole the size of a water buffalo was ripped from the bottom of his boat. A burning cigar held to her feet, he once tried to make her talk. He did not know that Evangelista was strutting on live coals from the first day she could walk and that her feet – as broad as dinner plates – were impervious to pain.

'Somewhere smilin' in the river,' said Evangelista, 'is a papa croc with a million dolla gut.' (But when in '98 I surface for the second time, Evangelista is dead. Rosada's men have taken her to the forest where, tied naked to a tree and smeared with honey, she is eaten alive by ants.)

In '88, Evangelista was very much alive and the proprietor of the Palace Caboose, the most unusual bordello in the hemisphere. She'd started off in a fancy train-car filled with trunks of French silk camisoles, stockings and scotch – gifts from Pedro II who was wild about her. Over the years she added forty mahogany-panelled rooms and a theatre where the Amazon-Junction Chamber Music Society performed and once the fabulous Sarah Bernhardt. The Palace Caboose had electricity ten years before the city, a modern kitchen and a rubber roof. Laotse, the Chinese cook (and the best cook in Brazil) had taught the girls how to use starch and how to fold the linen dinner napkins into fancy shapes: pagodas and cat's heads with pointy ears and galleons, and how to dice the meat and vegetables for the phoenix-rolls.

The Palace Caboose faced the river and the master bedroom had a spectacular view. The rain-proof roof was Evangelista's idea. The clay tiles, all dipped in hot latex, had never quite dried and within a week had trapped an example of every insect within forty square kilometres. Cletis Twigger, the American entomologist, had spent three months up there lying on a ladder. When he came down he offered to take Evangelista to Massachusetts where he was chairman of his department. Evangelista listened as he described the quiet life of the faculty wife, the graduation dinners and trustee teas, the gay alumni weekends when generous meals of Maine lobster, Great-Neck clams, broiled chickens and corn-on-the-cob oozing butter were served on green lawns upon long, stalwart tables illuminated by paper lanterns supplied by the faculty nursery school. He described the fine library that boasted over fifty thousand volumes (it had not occurred to him that Evangelista could not read), the pink granite dining-commons, the small, but well stocked museum which housed the largest collection of coprolites in the world (the finest he had donated himself). And he extolled the many virtues of his admirable colleagues: Olympus Cragg, the college president, had written a book on phenomenology.

But Evangelista, who had been born and bred in Belem and

in whose veins the Amazon's turgid waters surged, demurred. She admitted to me that, had Cletis Twigger been less fragile, she might have been tempted. But he was, she explained slyly, as dry as an empty coffin and his many, many allergies, aggravated by the tropical air, had afflicted him with a chronic cold. A drop of clear mucus permanently suspended from the tip of his thin nose had despoiled his vision of Heaven and subverted his courtship.

All this she told me at table, over one of the strangest meals I'll ever eat. Laotse had prepared a *peixada*, or Amazonian *bouillabaisse*. Among other things it contained yellow-fleshed *paçus* and red-fleshed *piracanjubas*. He had also stewed up a *bœuf bourgignon* but, short on beef, had stewed a sloth. Our dessert, served with a coulis of mango, was a teat-shaped pudding made with the eggs of an ibis and the milk of a manatee. Evangelista wore a green silk dress which I removed in time for the salad. She is the only woman I have ever seen whose nipples were blue. As we ate, we heard the laughter and the sighs of amorous couples in adjoining rooms. Now, that was a woman who knew how to entertain.

Not all my time in São José was spent frolicking in Evangelista's powerful arms. I was preparing to enter and explore an appendix-shaped sliver of dense, tropical forest that lies between the Amazon and the Japurà rivers. There was much talk of emerald deposits north-west of this region, but stones – even precious ones – have never captured my imagination.

Between the rivers, proliferates a cylindrically stemmed vine, its green flowers grouped in panicules. The corolla is inserted at the extremity of an unusually long ovary. You see, it is *this* that has ignited my mind.

CHAPTER THREE

THE COLOUR OF COPULATION

Lamprias de Bergerac

From Evangelista's balcony and after love, I dream upon the forest that swells beyond the waters, a Venusian vista apparently formed of gigantic concretions of malachite. From afar, the forest is mamilliform and mineral, her colours borrowed from the chemist's shelves: boron (the stuff that makes emeralds aquamarine) and copper; cobalt, iron, lead sulphide. And later, when I pierce her bubbles with my little boat, the scenery appears to be all freshly painted metal cut-outs, the stage props of my childhood Christmas theatres. But when I disturb the stainless steel backs of swimming snakes and come to rest beside her bearded banks, chemical and mineral collapse beneath the despotism of Queen Rubber and all her synthetic half-sisters: Vinyl and Velon, Celluloid and Cellophane. I mean to say the forest – stiff, elastic, robust and shimmering, *seasonless* – is too good to be true. It stretches like nylon cables to Heaven.

As in an alchemical drawing, the sun radiates from within a crown of clouds. My steamboat's copper prow halves the foaming water. The water, black and red, ripples with fish. I am visible at a great distance: a white cloud straying above the trees, a restless spirit. The forest appears to be drowning.

Dreaming and drowning. Eden embraces beauty and danger with equal passion: yellow orchids suspended in the air like clusters of bees but also mygales and *souroucoucou*, poisons that detonate in the blood; the fragrances of forgetfulness, of paranoia, of Paradise.

Imagine silences as beneath a bell of glass shattered by the clatter, chatter, twitter, croak and screech, tin drum rattle and lilting zither of insects swarming like galaxies. Imagine dangling profusions of shocking pink fingers that might be the phalluses of moonmen but are the ovaries of flowers. In every tree monkeys as numerous as leaves and birds as rain. Birds! Everywhere their flittings: whirrs of indigo and blazing crimson.

The first evening I bathe in one of the forest's silver streams and catch my dinner – fresh-water lobsters tucked under cold stones. I tie my hammock to the trees and, swathed in netting, hang as tranquilly as a cocoon, surrounded by snoring sloths. In the middle of the night I am awakened by the sound of a large animal drinking. Even now, an invisible tongue lapping, and the acridhoney smell of fur continue to haunt me, like the memory of a love affair.

When I was a boy, a very long time ago (for I am like an old, crusty *popóro* gourd, my avid, ancient poker points ever more insistently to Paddy Toadall's Funeral Home just down the road) I often lay flat against the grass and tried to imagine just what the world was like from the point of view of an ant. And now, here I am rocking beside grasses twice as high as myself and trying to ignore the oversize spiders.

But just what *is* a memory? When I summon that little boy, I recall not so much the grass, the sunlight heating my scalp, nor the hour, *but what it felt like to be an ant.* The spikygreen blades towering on all sides, and the fear of sudden death by squashing. Above all the sentiment of being much too small. My own memory is not what was, but what was felt.

The whispered words: *as small as* belong to my mother. They tickle my ear whenever I hear something buzz. Her perfume will always be associated in my mind with ants.

Now I am kicking up a smell, volatile and weird. I am

breathing the Amazon's intensely purple earth, a fearless admixture: the dung of jaguars, the blood of parrots, the horn of turtles, the milk of trees; milk, blood and dung all fused and fragmented by mushrooms and mandibles. This earth smells rich and sharp and clean and hearty. It smells like an Aztec's cup of hot cocoa. I exult: by what mysterious rite of sympathetic magic did such a soil give birth to cinnamon and chocolate?

I am not a botanist by profession, but an enamoured amateur. I am naive and expect to find a primitive micro-world, a mirror in which to contemplate the reflection of the Archetypal Idea. Instead, I see the future in flowers, which like angels or astronauts spend their entire existence in the sky. Their airborne roots are fitted with spongeous sails that soak up the rain as it falls. The primary elements – heavy and simple – have been transformed into the airy, the complex. Here I understand the true intent of Eden.

As I cut through the forest's sweet waters, the names of the Palace Caboose whores ring in my mind like a nursery rhyme:

Carol-Cul-Blanc
Tarantula-Jane
Tro-picale-Marquise!

The waters smell of musk and I hear crocodiles croaking like frogs the size of cows. Their pool and its lustrous debris is concealed behind curtains of vines. As I pass, the reptiles slam into the water, and, like Carol Cul Blanc dancing in her leather and her veils, garlands undulate, rising and falling in the waves.

Papa crocs eat their offspring when they get the chance and I cannot help but think that, had I devoured my own son Septimus as he lay writhing beneath the cawl, I would have done a Holy Thing . . .

Tarantula Jane? Here grows an orchid that imitates a spider with such sorcery, the male, seduced by the painted eyes of a lady who is not there but a *trompe l'œil* of pigment and wax, scurries mad with desire upon the flower, his fire dampened only when he discovers that his chosen bride has no sexual orifice. And perhaps you will not believe me, but in this incessant ocean of leaves, I see orchids that *have* that orifice, I see the spider copulate and come, see sperm glisten on her rigid tongue. If it seems perverse to you, as it does to Septimus my son, that flowers should choose to embrace another species and vice versa, I hasten to add that, if the insects inseminate their own kind a few yards further on, the blossoms are always faithful and take no other lover. Exhausted by the violence of the encounter and fertile, they quickly fade and die.

Septimus, jealous of my love for plants, despised them all. He attempted to justify this hatred when he insisted that plants, the whores of the natural world, fornicate with whatever comes their way: the wind, bugs, bats, birds, bees, snails, slimes and even men. In fact, the beauties of Evangelista's Palace were far more promiscuous – if less adventurous – for they copulated only with members of their own species.

My son had a morbid hatred of females, and whores in particular. Whores, like orchids, are the female archetype *par excellence*: painted, scented, seductive. Beneath their masks, the women of the Palace were fragile, luscious and unique. But the men who visited them were so blinded by lust they never saw what was there, only what was painted there.

This memory shines with the green light of the Devil's fertile lantern. Green is the colour of chlorophyll, the colour, therefore, of oxygen. And oxygen is the element that precipitated the animal kingdom.

'The colour of copulation,' says Cûcla, 'is green.'

Cûcla's people came originally from the mouth of the Amazon where the river and the sea meet with such intensity they create a bar of water that cannot be breached. This place is sacred. Here one may witness the First Manifestation: Sweet Water penetrating Salt Water. Here is the Primal Place of Copulation. It is Eternal. He who looks upon it is made wise – the possessor of spirit and logos.

Cûcla's word for forest means Perfumed Garden. And like the Greek *ouranos*, her word for palate is also the word for sky. The sky holds the Perfumed Garden in its mouth.

'The Universe,' says Cûcla, reaching for a stick of cool charcoal, 'looks like this . . .' And on her inner thigh she draws a boa, in the shape of a vulva, its tail in its mouth, circumscribing stars. Yet, when I say, 'Do you believe that there is a real snake in the sky?' she, crouching on her tiny feet, the feet of a child with the opaline nails cut to the quick, hoots with laughter.

'The snake is only an *idea*,' she teases, 'and like all good ideas He expands.' And bending she reaches for my nipple with her berrypink tongue, and the snake, waking, shakes himself and expands, just as she has promised.

I do not, for the sake of the tale, tread a straight path, but the snake's meandering path. I shall pass on to you a certain truth Cûcla taught me: that the straight path leads to a door of lead; it is the tortuous path that leads to the garden.

And this: only foolish men worship a god who banishes his children from Paradise. It is the fertile serpent who has the green thumb.

CHAPTER FOUR

FIRST EMBRACE

Septimus de Bergerac

The French word for life is *vie*; in English it means to strive for superiority. Had Darwin been less of a fool I might have admired him. However, I thank him for giving birth, if unwittingly, to Gobineau, the author of the *Essai sur l'inégalité des races humaines*.

I grew up a namer of names, a defamer, in short: a Patriot. From 1940–1944, I wrote nine hundred and twelve letters to the authorities. The virtuous Virginie de Fourtou, whom P'pa had left for a shell-sucking savage and a fist full of rotten vegetables, brought her son up to be a humble engineer of her race's victory. Had the war lasted a year or two longer, that victory would have been ours and Europe flushed forever of the Rabbi Republican rabble. It was Hitler's defeat and not P'pa's infidelity that broke her generous heart.

P'pa liked to pretend that evil is the result of an error, a species of cosmic bungle. Whereas I know it to be cosmic necessity, the force that binds the anarchic impulses of the galaxy. In other words, what P'pa calls Evil is Order.

In his later years, P'pa spent all his time tinkering with God's laws with all the blind conceit of the born heretic. He wanted to create living cells free of flaw. Which reminds me of Dust's fairy stories of True Man's namesake, who could enter water without getting wet and fire without getting burned. Unlike the Gypsy-Jews I sent down the road who, God be praised, burned easily.

P'pa created aberration. How could it be otherwise? When I got a glimpse of the dank forests he kept tucked away under glass, my bowels contracted in terror and disgust. It was a satanic tangle, the orifice of a giantess. And as I trampled and kicked and with my canes smashed the walls, sending glass raining down upon the immaculate emerald of his lawns and paths of gold brick, I felt happy for once, and powerful. An armoured tank in the Land of Oz.

True Man and I grew up in the family house in Angers on the Rue Monsecret. Its foundations had been laid in 1650 by our notorious ancestor, the heretic, libertine, jailbird and – as legend has it – alchemist, Savinien de Cyrano de Bergerac. His portrait hangs in the library: a small, dry-point engraving of a fat-nosed, fat-lipped, shifty-eyed individual with too much hair, whose resemblance with P'pa is striking. A monumental *armoire*, black as pitch, bears his crest: *Ici est la Sagesse*. In it M'man keeps the family's official papers – deeds, birth and death certificates – and the jewellery: a ruby ring rolled in the fist of a lace glove, like a frozen drop of Jewish blood, a pearl necklace, a finely executed Italian cameo depicting an unidentifiable figure draped in a Greek mode, an amber rosary, some Touareg silver from the Sahara, a gold locket containing one snipped curl of a dead infant's auburn hair gone green (this belongs to P'pa's dead brother Christian who fell down a well at the age of three), a spectacular set of bamboo and ivory mahjong in mint condition, a rare piece of obscenely carved pink jade and P'pa's photograph album.

I am seven years old and P'pa is side-stepping snakes in the selva. Mémé, M'man's strabismic mother, her ears plugged with pus, has moved in. If this is possible, she resents Dust even more than does M'man. True Man she refuses to acknowledge.

Mémé is as attached to her little Septimus-ti-ti as a Chinaman to his pigtail. (Her joke.) She is a bald, sombre person with a delicate but stupid head and the slopwise eyes of a maniac. I wonder: How can M'man be Mémé's daughter? Then again, Mémé is a Métro and not a de Fourtou.

Mémé tries at once to convince M'man to wean me, for I continue to take nourishment from the maternal teats. In this way, for all these years, Virginie Grenier de Fourtou de Bergerac has killed my lusty appetite and the tedious time.

Mémé subscribes to a monthly magazine called *The Public Good*. And she writes numerous letters to the editors:

September 12, 1888

Dear Sir,

I want my grandson to consume only eggs that are very fresh. Please indicate a serious and simple procedure by which I will be permitted to know the veritable freshness of the eggs which are sold to the public, often erroneously, as 'freshly laid eggs'.

My distinguished salutations
Bergeronnette Métro

The editor's reply is published along with her letter in the October issue of *The Public Good*.

. . . Drop the egg (or eggs) into a large bottle of salt-water. (12 grams of salt for 2 litres of water.) A fresh egg will fall to the bottom.

Thereafter, M'man never goes to market without the wide-necked bottle of salt-water plugged with a piece of cloth and a cork. And I, my face pinched in an expression of distrust, hold her hand. *And I carry the bottle.* It is just possible that, swollen by my own importance, I carry the bottle in an attitude of precocious pomposity. There is a photograph of myself from that period, looking grave beyond my years. After all, I had become the man of the house.

M'man never goes to market without a handkerchief imbued with 'Essence Algérienne' held to her nose. Mémé, squat, squinting, squeamish with gout, emphysema and varicose veins, stays at home. I do not pity the Poultry-Egg and Poultry Man who visibly winces when he sees us.

I hate the bustle of the market, housewives pullulating like roaches in a synagogue, and yet I do admire M'man's ability to select a firm, ripe cheese, a delicately marbled slice of beef and I know how to test a melon for ripeness by pulling off the stem and pressing the underpart and holding it to my lips. The smell of a ripe melon, even now, reminds me of my M'man.

In the evening, I sit with Mémé on M'man's knees at the dining-room table. The dishes have been cleared away, and Mémé and M'man sip cordials. Sometimes True Man is there as well, sitting in Mademoiselle Parfait's angular lap. Mémé always ignores him. She spreads the latest edition of *The Public Good* out upon the table and entertains us with stories of Francis II's adenoids, the senile gangrene of Louis XIV, Ann of Austria's cancer and the attempted suicide of Napoleon I. The people of France, warns *The Public Good*, are threatened by Racial Contamination. Mémé stops reading and stares meaningfully at Mademoiselle Parfait. She drags True Man, squalling and kicking, upstairs to his mother. He protests because he wants to hear the rest. The rest is vague, however; stimulating, and mouthwatering, but in no way can it be called satisfying. To ensure the future of my race (and not True Man's, Mémé reminds me unnecessarily) *The Public Good* hints of a mysterious programme that will, in the not too distant future, be set into motion, should it find the unequivocal support of the People of France. Anyone concerned by the welfare of their country must continue to subscribe to *The Public Good*.

Before sleep, in the intimacy of M'man's bedroom, I clasp

her breasts with both hands and squeeze. M'man is a fountain. Making an 'O' with my mouth, I catch the warm milk as it spurts forth. Its whiteness fills me, whitens my breath, my spirit, my skin. I dally thus for nearly an hour and I make a great quantity of noise: sucking and smacking, cupping her breasts in my palms and bouncing them. These are happy times. But the following week I am weaned upon Mémé's insistence.

Shortly thereafter, Mémé suffers a stroke for which I, having prayed incessantly for her death, feel responsible. She sits haggard and helpless in a pierced chair; a dreadful stench drifts about her skirts. I sit in her lap only because M'man says I must, wishing for just this once to change places with True Man. Mémé holds me tightly. All her remaining strength is concentrated in her fingers. I fear that it is her intention to snap me up with her three licorice-stained teeth and shell my skull like a pea.

'There was once a little boy named Septimus who was no bigger than a needle with a head like a pea and whose Papa had gone to sea . . .'

I squirm and look desperately at the parlour door.

'Look into my eye!' she pinches my arm, 'when I am telling you a story!'

I look into her crazy eye and see myself floating there.

'That's better. That's bé, bé, bé . . .' Mémé's grip tightens and pulling me to her she falls asleep. I stiffen and try to slip away. I squirm and I sob, I even plead, but Mémé sleeps on. An hour passes. The parlour is as silent as a tomb. She is so cold I begin to shiver. At last Mademoiselle Parfait comes into the room with a lamp. My teeth are chattering.

'Your Mémé is dead,' Mademoiselle decides at once. 'I'll go and get your mother.' It is true. Mémé's eyes, milky and vitreous, have turned blue.

The doctor breaks her arms to free me. P'pa, who is the Devil knows where, carousing on beaches with negresses or fornicating in a filthy steamer on the Rio Negro with a monkey, is not on hand for the funeral.

CHAPTER FIVE

CESTE PIERRE EST VEGETALE

Lamprias de Bergerac

Christmas Eve, 1891. A disaster! Foolishly I expect my family to be pleased to see me. I've been away three years. I bring gifts of guava paste, pineapple, coconut caramels and a cage full of turquoise parakeets. But Virginie and I fight like polecats, and Dust, her mind already dipping (and for this I will never forgive myself) has developed a morbid fascination for words starting with the letter O and chatters ominously about obituaries, ossuaries and obstructions. True Man is so in awe of me that he hides behind his mother's skirts and cannot be tempted by the exotic sweets. And the precociously malevolent Septimus has burned my most beloved books; in the centre of the library floor a great charred circle is all that remains of this infant scoundrel's first *auto da fé*. It is more than fortunate that the sinister Septimus did not destroy a small but precious manuscript written and illuminated by my ancestor, Savinien de Cyrano de Bergerac. The quintessence of his short life's work, it was kept where I myself had discovered it – tucked in a hollow panel beneath the *armoire*'s crest.

That night after a stunningly silent meal, and doubtless to shame and to punish me, Virginie admits to an affair with her masseur, the ludicrous Kindergarten. I have the temerity to tell her about Evangelista. She throws a fit and languishes for hours on the bedroom carpet, sobbing. My elbows deep in imaginary fuchsias, I lie in our bed alone, conjuring up visions of mangroves. When she stops crying, I try to describe for her the scarlet ibis gathered by the hundreds and leaning with their elegant beaks together towards the green-complexioned backwaters. She stuns me by howling obscenities. I think: I must return at once to the land of the toucan and the kinkajou! The land of the monkey-trees and the docile manatees!

A light snow is falling. I dress warmly in my jungle-cat vest, take up my Brazilian hat, my favourite walking stick, my leather bag (its soiled linens still unpacked) and make a short visit to the *armoire* where I fish Savinien's manuscript from its hiding place and slip it safely into an inner pocket. As I walk down the stairs I hear Virginie wailing and pounding on the floor with her fists. Dust, appearing on the third floor landing, peers down at me. 'Outlaw,' she says. 'Outsider.'

'Orchids,' I explain.

So I leave my home, forever, on Christmas morning. Already I am dreaming of my own Mesopotamia, my valley of hanging gardens and siren-infested waters. I am an Amazonian: arboreal and aquatic. I swim with jaguars and deer; I sleep, like the sloth, hanging from a tree.

From Angers I take the morning train to Paris where I book passage on a ship that leaves for Rio on the first of January. Then a hansom cab takes me to Neuilly where I spend the week with my old friend the eminent chemist and botanist, Angelo Mariani.

Angelo's home, with its opulent ceilings, stairwells, mirrored walls and precious carpets, is the most sumptuous I know. Above all, his beautiful glass-vaulted arboreta contain the world's most expensive domestic plantations of coca. Unlike my wife, Angelo greets me with enthusiasm. The year before I had sent him an account of my studies of the Amazonian flora, describing *en passant* the luxuriously-leafed species of coca encountered in the limited region of my exploration. Since we last spoke together, his beard and hair have turned white. But he is still brilliant, handsome, magnetic. In the enchanted twilight of his study, seated in chairs carved with the coca motif and beneath the ceiling's superb views of jungle beasts in deadly combat, we savour a fine green tea of Andean coca and talk. I have, as always in his rooms, the soothing impression of being one thousand miles from Paris and at the farthest extremity of the earth.

'So! You are back from the arms of the Amazon . . . And have you seen the ants as large as foxes and the bees as big as bats?'

'Everything is bigger there, and better!'

'Except for the coca, *n'est-ce pas?*' And, flashing a dazzling smile, he shows me a small bronze 'Coca Nymph' by Rivière, crowned with the familiar leaves.

Coca is for those who seek not oblivion, but exhilaration. Neither is it a hallucinogen, but, as it frees the blood of uric acid, it banishes fatigue. After tea, I admire Angelo's breathtaking collection of Incan erotic pottery. The burnished image of a handmaiden on her knees sucking her lord's erect phallus sends me into a rigid fit of longing for my passionate Evangelista. He has also acquired a rare copy of Frampton's translation of Nicolas Monardes' 1565 publication, *Joyful News of the Newe Founde Worlde, Wherein is Declared the Virtues of Hearbes, Trees, Oyales, Plantes and Stones.*

Monardes describes the coca plant beautifully:

'. . . The leaves, somewhat like myrtle, but larger and more succulent and green . . .'

'Speaking of succulence . . .' Angelo hands me a leaf – olive green, translucent, with an aroma to conjure angels – and some lime.

The leaf is well cured, but still contains just enough moisture; glossy and pliable, it is from the region of Yunges, Peru, and its flavour is incomparable: *coca del dia*! This, Angelo cannot grow. The plants need the high, dry reaches of the Andes. Altitudes of 3,000 to 4,000 metres produce the finest leaves and even the best artificial soil – a savant mixture of leaf mould and sand – cannot replace the Andean red clay. I ask him about Amazonian coca, 'Mama Coca'. I learn that, although the shrubs are more prolific in the warm, moist atmosphere of the valley, the alkaloidal yield is greatly inferior. To a manufacturing chemist such as he, the best coca is that which yields the greatest percentage of crystallizable cocaine. However, as the Indians know well, this same leaf is to be shunned for domestic consumption. The leaves richest in cocaine are bitter; the leaf-eaters select the sweet, 'poorer' leaves.

Later on in the evening, after an exquisite meal of roast pheasant stuffed with shallots and chestnuts and an excellent Château Brane-Cantenac bottled in 1811 (the year, Angelo reminds me, of the Comet), I decide to show him my precious manuscript. The leather is so old it looks frosted and the pages, covered with an eccentric hand in crimson ink, are of stiff, cream-laid paper. The marbled end-papers, scarlet, gold and green, are intact. And now I will set down for you as best I can from memory, those prophetic words and images that so transformed my life.

The first page, written with flourish, Angelo recognizes at once as a quote from the *Table Smaragdine*.

'It begins very well,' he says, 'for when I transform my coca into crystals of cocaine I . . .'

separate earth and fire, the subtle and the dense, gently and with great care.

'And look here!' I turn the page, unable to contain my excitement.

CESTE PIERRE EST VEGETALE

'Have you ever before, in all your years of study, seen the philosopher's stone defined as vegetal?'

'Never.'

Above this uncanny phrase, so thrilling to us both, and drawn in my ancestor's nervous hand, is the image of the swimmer who, as any student of alchemy knows, is a metaphor for fish and, therefore, for the Christ. But Savinien's image, unlike any other we have ever seen, floats head down, his hair fanning out from the cranium—

'Like roots.'

'If you turn the page,' I say to Angelo, 'you will see why I chose tonight, after your excellent Château Brane-Cantenac, to show you my treasure.' And now the second image comes to light: a blazing comet, its 'hair' fanning out like the hair of the swimmer.

'Of course,' Angelo need not remind me, 'the latin *cometa* means: the hairy. And curiously, the comet is the metaphor for nucleus. And, if our swimmer is no swimmer, but instead – a drowned man? *Un noyé. Un noyau.* A *nucleus*, my dear Lamprias.' He is thoughtful.

'A cell. Could this be a vast metaphor for parthenogenesis? The Immaculate Conception?' But, if we have come so far so fast, the rest is woven of obscure parabole, 'moonless midnight,' says Angelo.

Sheepishly, I admit that, in all the years I have pondered over this curious inheritance, it had never occurred to me that it described a biological process. Angelo teases me when he insists that all the references to *ore* refer not to gold but to orchids . . .

'What,' I ask Angelo, 'is *nigrum, nigrus, nigro* – blacker than black?'

'The alchemists believed that black contains all colours. Perhaps it is a metaphor for fecundity.'

'Black earth?'

'You do know the root of the word: alchemy?'

'*Al-Kmi*. The Dark Land. Meaning Egypt. But what does Egypt have to do with drowning men? Falling stars? The Exodus?'

'My friend Lamprias,' Angelo laughs, 'always prone to wanderlust. You wander too far. We know your ancestor is not concerned with corpses nor with comets – but with *living cells*. If the stone is vegetal, it needs to be nurtured. Your Amazonian earth is the adamic earth. Perhaps you will find the answer there.'

We toast to this with an astonishing 'wine' made from the choice leaves of the Caravaya district. Rich in cocaine, it has a bitter, musty taste, but contains all the virtues and benefits of the leaf. And when, at the week's end, he insists that I take a supply with me, I board ship with my bag far heavier than when I left home, filled as it is with bottles of the very same 'liquor' Pope Leo XIII has hanging from his neck and that the French soldiers will carry close to their hearts in the trenches of the First World War. I later wondered if it was thanks to Angelo's wine that I was able to count over two hundred species of mosquito, from Belem to São José, without once being stung.

When I was a boy of twelve and interested in frogs and nests and minerals, my father, a gentleman and a dreamer who spent his adult life tearing his own unfinished poems to shreds, took me to Paris where we visited the museum of palaeontology. And there, among ghosts too crippled to ascend Heaven, I lost my innocence.

Earlier, we had been to the zoo and had seen a mature orang-outang (or as the Malays call him, man of the woods) sobbing silently in a corner of his cage. He was my first lesson in old age. One look at his body seized in an eternity of suppressed desire, and I was no longer a careless boy contemplating a curiosity. Even now, I ache for both of us; a species who can so deprive another is to be pitied. But the full extent of our tragedy became evident only after I had entered the museum. It taught me – if wordlessly (for I was still too young to name my intuitions) – that the species to which I belong is damned.

The first floor exhibit entitled 'Compared Anatomy' contains a startling collection of monsters. I was so taken with these that for a few, long moments I forgot the suffering ape. The tiny, brittle skeleton of Siamese twins ignited the dry air with the impact of a small stellar explosion. Helen and Philomène are so joined that the shared orbit of their pelvis, from which only three legs sprout, forms a shocking triskelion of bone. They are flanked by others like themselves – if smaller and yellower – and guarded by an infant cyclops who hangs from his wire like a key to the gates of Nightmare.

Here I saw babies born with beaks, with tails, hooves, the faces of goats; a six-legged lamb and the ears of twelve murdered chimpanzees. The flayed, eagle-spread body of a young orang-outang offers organs so like my own that I cannot help but wonder if the day will come when men, in the name of Science, will so violate the bodies of other men. I fear that I will also be reduced to dreaming in a jar, the thin slices of my penis stained blue and displayed – like the elephant's – beneath a lens.

Even then, it was evident to me that a science which creates such havoc in order to proceed is not a True Science. And I prayed I might come to understand the intimate structures of life without this abject tampering. The great room and its marvels stank of poverty.

Father and I then moved quickly on, past the majestic

Megaptère Boops and Austral Whale (creatures now near extinct and said to converse in opera and philosophy) and went up the marble stairs to the second storey where the bird-hipped Hypsilophodon high-stepped in his glass case and the lizard-hipped Brontosaur lumbered with all the fabulous weight of his unfathomable antiquity. I felt more at ease among these creatures metamorphosised into minerals and freed from the grip of time. Here was a clean science. Yet their still abstractions chilled me. When we left the museum to find the world outside shining topaz in the late afternoon sun, I was overjoyed to see the chestnut trees sagging with nuts and the winged seeds of maples scattered everywhere. The hot, happy blood of boyhood sent me bounding across the forbidden grass.

My father, delighting in my sudden change of mood, said something startling and amusing about our 'infernal voyage' and the 'ritual murders of impotent men'. Never have I loved him more. 'Some men,' he liked to say, 'are seduced by the promises of demons.' Now he said: 'We have visited a curiously coloured nightmare, Lamprias, and the burial grounds of dragons. Now we shall visit the city's daydream of Eden.' And he took me to Paris's winter gardens, where tropical palms rise forty metres to a crown of tinted glass and where even the air is made of gold dust and chlorophyll. When we entered the maze of greenhouses where a thousand, thousand leaves and blossoms trembled beneath an artificial rain, I took his hand gratefully and squeezed it to thank him for the answer he had given me: Botany.

Perhaps, one day, you will visit a greenhouse and see plants reproduced *in vitro*. The cells, all exact replicas of the mother cell, float like tiny, seeded pearls in their miniature oceans. Here is the swimmer of Savinien's manuscript – the meristem – germinating in a nourishing culture. My first such culture contained sea-water and coconut milk, sterilized in Cûcla's *bain-marie*. And, fifty years later, my cymbidiums flourish in calcium nitrate, phosphate of potassium; magnesium, ammonium and iron sulphates, agar, distilled water and sugar.

When, in 1902, I surfaced from the Amazon for the second time, hairy, tattered and happy – and with Cûcla in my shadow – I found waiting for me in the desolation of the Palace Caboose, a fly-specked cablegram from Angelo. A German scientist named Haberlandt had kept minute masses of plant cells alive in an artificial environment for several months. This confirmed the intuition which – born of those years of dream and reflection – had evolved into certitude as I sat in the tree-tops among monkeys gathering the seeds of orchids in the sky.

I have said that Cûcla walked in my shadow when in fact I walked in hers. She wore the Amazon's eternal evening like a mantle and, even after we had made our home in rooms that were flooded with sunlight – even in the midst of winter when the snow's reflection shimmied on the walls – still did she tread the adamic earth, the gravity of her innocence forcing me to confront a fear, darker than dark, that having found Her at last, I should lose Her. But here I am, once again, getting ahead of myself!

In the winter of 1892, I returned to São José in time to celebrate Evangelista's birthday. The Palace Caboose was as gorged with fruits and flowers as a cornucopia. Dressed in a skirt of bananas, Carol Cul Blanc did a three-hour samba about a ming soup tureen filled twelve times to the brim with sparkling *chicha*. When she was finally carried off kicking by the Minister of Finance, whose erection had breached his fly with the ferocity of an angered bull, Evangelista, now forty-two years of age and as fragrant as a ripe *poupougne*, challenged

Tarantula Jane to a contest of songs. They sat opposite one another in the centre of the room, among the skins and pips of fruits and empty bottles, Jane, her fabulous red hair studded with flowers and Evangelista, her *cafuso*'s complexion as glossy in the candlelight as the skin on a bowl of milk, their banjos balanced on their rosy knees. And so clever were they, so delightful and inventive were their songs, that a tie was proclaimed, and I, as horny as Zeus himself, got to take them both to bed where they lay embracing, as I, a bee between two orchids, visited with my tongue and then my stinger, each swollen set of vulval lips and in such tender confusion, that soon I no longer knew whose lips were whose nor where I was; nor did they seem to know themselves, or care.

CHAPTER SIX

THE TWO-HUNDRED-METRE BATTERY

Lamprias de Bergerac

Doubtless you are wondering what had precipitated my marriage with Virginie, when it is evident that I was made to wander alone, to follow intuition's thin, glimmering thread where it would lead me.

We were introduced at a garden party. The women all fiddled with fans, and the men, their moustaches carefully waxed, stood about as stiffly as their own starched collars. In evanescent brocade, Virginie, a 'bibi' of tulle and whalebone perched smartly on her head, was a wonderfully long-waisted girl with large, astonished eyes and thick, black eyebrows, close set, like centipedes about to copulate. Her lips, as they folded over a creamcake, were the colour of apricots and for one wet instant divulged her tongue. She sipped her tea and silently accepted another cake. Enchanted, I watched as it too disappeared into her mouth and down a throat noosed with pearls.

'Virginie!' bellowed my mother, in taffeta, with me in tow. 'My son is only just returned from the turbulence of the Guianan jungle!' And she backed off ostentatiously, leaving us alone. Virginie, her great blue irises ringed with darker indigo fixing a mysterious distance on the horizon just beyond my left ear, whispered dreamily, '*The voyager . . . The voyager pursues his road, free and contented. He possesses nothing yet the entire world is at his feet. His eyes are ceaselessly struck by new objects which give him food for thought. Our life,* don't you think . . .' and for the first time she looked into my eyes, '*our life is a voyage.*'

Head over heels in love I proposed to her within the week. My mother, delighted by the prospect of my domestication, gave the de Bergerac ancestral house over to wall-paperers, and retired to one of the family's many country estates where she lived piously and in the company of harassed housemaids, and where she produced twenty-four night-bonnets and a linen altar cloth before passing on.

It was not until the ordeal of our honeymoon that I was forced to admit that my bride, for all her fetching ways with pastry, and despite the heavenly bliss of her eyes, had no soul. O! The memory of that week in Hell! Unable to bed her – for the sight of my naked body had shocked her into a froth of loathing – I attempted to talk to her. But my Virginie had no mind; her conversation was only what she had managed to memorize from her exercise books. I remember the morning of my awakening . . .

We were walking down a freshly raked path fragrant with jasmine. I commented upon the smell.

'*Perfume*,' said Virginie, '*is agreeable to the nose. The shade*,' she added, '*is agreeable to those who walk.*' I mentioned Darwin.

'*Books*,' said my wife interrupting me, '*are agreeable to the wise.*' Our path led to a tearoom. I suggested refreshment. When our cakes and coffee were served, Virginie, brushing an éclair with the apricot lips I already loved less, said:

'*The most agreeable coffee comes from Arabia.*'

'Virginie, dearest . . .' I took her small, gloved hand in mine, '*talk* to me, dearheart.'

'I *am* talking! Yes . . . and that reminds me: *The conversation of the ignorant is insipid*, don't you think?'

I then asked her why she had consented to be my wife. Virginie tore a brioche in two and buttered it tenderly. 'My mother bade me marry,' she explained, taking a bite, 'and I

51

did.' She brushed crumbs from her blouse. '*Youth takes council from the aged.*'

By the end of the week the marriage was still not consummated. At dinner I suggested an annulment. And there in the hotel dining room, surrounded by elderly couples in retirement, a baked custard quivering in its dish beneath her eager spoon, Virginie threw herself into a fit of shrieking, the first fit of the Feast of Fits which was to punctuate our life together.

'If only,' said Virginie, once we returned home and her mother had convinced her that she was, like all mortal women, sexual, 'if only people could reproduce photographically.' Even this *bon mot* was not her own, but belonged to Dr Roux, the eccentric inventor of the two-hundred-metre high battery, and then at the apex of fashion.

The week following our honeymoon, I left for China to study the *Aerides odoratum* and the *Arundina*, two particularly luscious specimens of orchids. I wanted to give my new bride time to accustom herself to the physical realities of marriage. Always an optimist, I imagined the slow awakening of desire, and passion's blossom. I hoped Virginie would come to miss me. I flattered myself that once having entered her mind I would enter her body. I never even considered what was to be Kindergarten's technique: to rub her neck, to rub her back, to massage her ribs and her buttocks, her thighs, her feet, her knees and then all over again – for an hour, for two hours – until her body, as elastic and as yeasty as teacake batter, would be ready for what she called: *The Sacrifice*.

Once and only once would this madwoman be mine and once was all she needed to conceive a Calamity.

And Dust? Dust I had pulled from the fire, only to drop her into Virginie's infernal frying pan. When I had found her sitting in the streets of Peking holding onto her little bleeding feet, banished by her mother-in-law for having stolen a peach, I chose to believe that Virginie, an obedient (if unbedded) wife and a devout Christian, would be pleased to adopt so needy, so self-effaced, so exotic a companion.

Dust was a dear, gentle thing and lovely when she smiled. I recognize that it was a blunder to get her pregnant. But so grateful was she for the kindness shown her, so anxious to please, that during our travels together she was forever posing herself in the most provocative postures, and giggling behind her plump hands in the most suggestive manner imaginable.

It was impossible for me to concentrate on my work. My head was swimming with visions of this doll-like creature, her legs like sharpened pencils in the air, her jewelled mouth a ripe fig seeded with teeth. As I fell into her bed I imagined for a fleeting, foolish instant my ancestor's dark, sprawling house transformed by two women living as sisters together, surrounded by an affectionate brood of children. And so, from foggy thinking fired by lust, I created a madhouse.

I reflected upon all this beneath a canopy of blossoming cattleyas; clusters of *Brassavola fragrans*, not visible to the eye, filled the air with savage sweetness. And I remembered that before setting himself down to his business of miracles, Savinien had needed to dispel the shadows that tempted his spirit and troubled his heart. He described his mood as one of Profound Melancholy. Reviewing my amorous history, myself heavy of heart, I felt closer to him than to any man I had ever known. I feared that I was a coward, I feared I was deluded, I feared I was, at best, a fool.

CHAPTER SEVEN

THE SPIRIT OF MERCURY

Lamprias de Bergerac

The Amazon abounds in limited populations of unique varieties. My chosen corner produced particularly stunning examples of *Brassavola fragrans*, *Epidendruns* and a curious miniature *Paphiopedilum*, or 'slipper of Venus'. Well worthy of the Goddess of love, her sepals were trimmed with purple fur.

In those days I favoured a dream of creating a decorative hybrid of *Vanilla planifolia* that would grow as a bush and not as a vine. With luck the tubers, packed carefully in moss, would survive the long journey back to Europe. I collected no animal specimens and so was unencumbered by the sinister, hollow skins of birds and mammals and the biscuitdry bodies of bugs – all subject to mould, bacteria and mites. I kept a metal locker in the steamboat for my notebooks, stored my precious orchid dust in tins, and, in the air, constructed the greenhouse of my dreams. I spent hundreds of hours in Paradise thinking about plumbing.

For a time, I was shadowed by a young male baboon. Attracted by the smell of roasting bananas, he once approached my fire and appeared prepared, at least for a spellbinding moment, to ramble over and join me in the feast. His prick, which he rallied as a flag when I first entered what must have been his territory, was a rainbow of ruby, purple and violet. I wrote to the ladies at the Palace about it. Jane replied: 'That vision has spoiled us for life. Last week the "King of Africa", Tombola, that gambling rascal, showed up to regale us ladies with his midnight tower, his ebony pony, his rod of black lightning. We all thought of your provocatively endowed neighbour and I fear our lack of enthusiasm hurt Tom's feelings. Evangelista says she was as excited as if it was but Twigger "touting his bent needle".

'P.S. We do so miss you, dear. Aren't you getting tired of all those pods and tubers and things? We fear a puma may snatch away our favourite piece – do you really walk around in the nude?'

I did. The only inconvenience was that the soles of my feet picked up chigger eggs which had to be poked out with the point of my knife.

Angelo had sent me several cases of his coca wine and I had never felt better. Mosquitoes and flies continued to ignore me. I have read accounts by explorers who talk of little else and I will never know if it was my own fortunate chemistry or Angelo's brew that protected me. Had the wine charmed my skin? He had slipped, into a case of bottles, a handsome, maroon volume with dry-point engravings of the famous people who swore by its magic: Nadar, H. G. Wells, Sarah Bernhardt, Rodin, to name but a few. Even Freud was seduced by Vin Mariani; it enabled him – a timid neurotic with a nervous stomach – to proclaim his passion to the woman he loved, and, according to Angelo, cleared the way to the stunning invention of psychoanalysis. Another one of my son's bugaboos! Years later Septimus would write in one of his many deadly books and pamphlets, texts which would feed the fire that consumed the Jews of France:

Psychoanalysis and the Theory of Relativity are the two primary perils of the Occident; both are the unscrupulous, purposeful deformations of logic and dangerous to French society and morality; both are the perfidious inventions of an alien mentality, the unstable mind of the Jew, the Semite, the Yid Rag Picker . . .

A pleasant three days' journey north-west up a quiet tributary took me to the peaceful *yano* of friendly Indians, where I was able to procure tobacco, manioc flour and fistfuls of brilliant feathers which, sent to São José by way of the Iquitos-Obidos mail route, reached destination: the deep, hot clefts of Jane's and Evangelista's marvellous bosoms.

I enjoyed my excursions to the *yano*. Living alone among the flowers imparted each visit with the colour and excitement of high adventure. And my spirit, anticipating Cûcla, was winging: swimming pigs, boiling fountains, fugitive deer – all dimly perceived in the sticky air – hinted that my *anima mundi* was near. Yet many weeks would pass before that miraculous meeting of eyes, that first molten flash of recognition.

The *yano* lay upon the forest like a colossal shell. The entire structure, elegant, oval and flooded with filtered light, was built of bamboo and smelled pleasantly like the attic of a hay barn.

Always I was greeted with laughter. My ponderous nose, my hairy body amused everyone. But this laughter was friendly and accompanied by the best they had: wiggly, white larva, butterysweet (like custard, in fact) or roasted ants – things I could never swallow without an exaggerated show of bravura which was accepted as a novel display of appetite. These Indians wore vanilla orchids in their nostrils and ears, and strings of the fragrant pods stirred at their necks. I was at home.

They also made a great cigar and a peerless banana beer, gourd rattles, turtleshell clappers and xylophones of bone. Here I saw, with the help of a few masterful strokes of soot, a pair of buttocks transformed into the startling face of a fish. Above all, these people made conversation; their conversation was nothing less than the orchestration of the jungle that pressed panting and whistling about the *yano*.

A cluster of *kê* sounds, made as the tongue slapped the base of the palate, hammered out the language's spine. It was joined by glottal catches in perfect imitation of a lizard's cry, rising to a strident, driving pitch before abruptly snapping off, like the lizard's tail. A joyous greeting, with its invitation to partake of beer and ants, incorporated the rhythmic thump of ripe *poupougnes* cascading to the ground, laughter and a malicious wink. (In the Amazon, each invitation to supper is an exercise in trust; some tribes are known to eat travellers.)

Each man, woman and child carried a fish-skin drum, a one-stringed harp, mouth-bow, flute or janglers, and I could never tell where the conversation ended and the music began. Daily life was an impromptu musical feast, the men squatting together chanting the familiar *kêkêkêkêkêkêkêkêkêkê* as the women and children, with the voices of ibises and angels, intoned a high-coloured melody that rebounded with spirit and sensuality upon the *kêkêkêkê*'s metallic, hypnotic trampoline.

Much later, when Cûcla (who, although I could not know it, was already there, hiding behind her mask of *roucou* and soot and her aunty's broad back) was to be talked into buying all sixty-eight varieties of household rubbish from the Fuller brush man – including eighteen brushes – she would eloquently plead, '. . . He knew all the words of the planet of bottles and brushes and scouring pads; all the flutters and twitters and gurgles and glissandos; baby, he sang the opera of pig-bristle and tortoise-shell and spun-sugar feather-duster! The man knew how to talk! How could I refuse him?'

'But Cûcla – all this junk!' And she, tears flowing into her open mouth:

'Damn! Lamprias! No one makes music here 'cept the radio!' And she runs to the greenhouse and there, crouching in its artificial rain sings her songs, and with a little aluminium pie-plate and a silver spoon beats out the song's backbone, a flat, miserable, lousyday *kêkêkêkêkêkêkêkê*!

Cûcla, then, hiding behind her aunty, was watching my attempts to communicate my friendliness and curiosity and gratitude to her tribe. My knowledge of that melodious language was meagre, but I threw myself into it and jollified my helplessness with whistles, jigs, hand-clappings and hoots. Cûcla, having recently come of age, and stealing peeks from behind her aunty's copper shoulder decided, God knows why, that I was just the sort of object she needed for a husband. Concealed by the naked aunty, her sisters and her pals, and amid giggles and whispers, she hatched her plot: that first she would follow me, haunt me with her child's games and nubile magic . . .

Like the Mystery of Savinien's manuscript, Cûcla revealed herself to me in winks and sparks.

One morning, not long after a visit to the *yano*, I was sitting on a pebble beach when a swarm of dragonflies materialized out of the fluid air and settled upon my body. I froze, nearly swooning with delight, when laughter chimed from the trees and I realized, as I spun about in a turmoil of sugary wings, that I had heard this laugh before, stifled, distant, but undeniably the same explosion of girlish mirth. I called out and was answered by the splash of a tortoise sliding from a hot stone into the cool water.

The next day, a thoughtless, thunderous fart, as I stretched in the treetops to reach spectacular blossoms of *planifolia*, inspired yet another fit of merrymaking. But when I traced it to a leafy tangle a few yards away and, with the lumbering efforts of a woolly-brained gorilla, managed to reach the branch where I could have sworn a coca nymph had been swinging naked from her hands an instant before, I found only a bunch of green *poupougnes*, too sour to eat.

That night I was awakened by the soft touch of a curious finger in my beard as I slept hung between the willows, and in the scattered light of the moon saw a slight, lithe figure, as nimble as a lutin, slip away into the shadows . . .

But it is I who surprised her, or so I like to think (she never satisfied my curiosity on this point, her answer only laughter or a kiss), when early one evening, prodded on by happy intuition, I followed a barely perceptible path, caught the smell of her fire, and saw – illuminated by the living embers, crouching on her little feet, her naked buttocks balancing like a firm, split mango just above the earth, the perfect curve of her dolphin back, the delicate neck of a songbird coyly cocked to one side, a wand of roasted iguana held smoking before her lips – Cûcla. Breathing upon the meat to cool it, she made sparks.

As she ate, she swayed from side to side, humming one of the rhythmic melodies so beloved of the Japura river tribes and talked to herself, or so I thought until I saw the marmoset mewing at her feet and toying with her toes. And then the marmoset saw me and, as it leapt up and down screaming, its fluffy tail bristled for battle, Cûcla raised herself and turned, her seraph's eyes igniting my soul. The marmoset, now clinging to one of her shapely legs, was apparently clammering every vile oath known in the language of marmosets.

Cûcla, seeing the lump of a fool that I was, my ungroomed beard put to shame by the monkey's tail, my nose imitating the tuberous root of the edible manioc, smiled, and I have never known why, what it was that had from the start attracted her, certainly not my gift for making thunder?

My heart leapt: she gave the marmoset a shake and a kick and threw a hot chunk of toasty iguana in my face. I fumbled, didn't catch it: her beauty had unstrung me, utterly. She giggled and pulled off another piece. This time I caught it.

Bravely, my arm outstretched, the meat burning my fingers, I went to her. She stretched her neck and tugged and nibbled and then playfully licked my hand, and we fed each other the rest of that *iguana deliciosa*. Then she proffered her lips – at the corner of which I saw glistening a speck of charred wood – and I fell delirious from a very high place, dizzy because I had found the woman of my life.

The marmoset, in a paroxysm of jealous rage, leapt about us screeching until Cûcla cuffed him smartly, sending him rolling into foetal position where, thank Heaven, he mumbled himself to sleep.

Trickster Cûcla! She couldn't have been more than twelve. And once we had become friends and had spent long weeks loving one another, she decided it was time to return to the *yano* to celebrate in style her hairy catch whose sexual prowess, prodded by her inventive shamelessness and infinite curiosity, surpassed (so I like to pretend) that of the most firmbodied (I hoped), sleek, young hunter-songster of her acrobatic tribe.

We chugged upriver and turned off into the shady tributary that led to the *yano*. We spent so much time making love or attempting to comprehend one another that it took us nearly five days to get there. We docked in a mangrove and set off into the forest. When we reached the familiar footpath, Cûcla leapt to my back and scrambled to my shoulders, hugging my head between her thighs. And in this jocular manner, Cûcla making more racket than a multitude of young monkeys, we reached the *yano*. But we heard no familiar song of welcome and we saw no smoke rising.

'Before the end of the world,' once said my wife Virginie over breakfast, as she filled her mouth with jam (and she was paraphrasing Dr Roux), 'the earth will be a mirror of Hell.' Hell was waiting for us, just around the road's turning, Hell and the end of the world. If there had been a warning of what we were to find, a warning written in the leaves, the mud, the sky – love had struck us both sightless.

At the entrance to the *yano* sprawled a child's skeleton. Within the inner courtyard, the bones of the entire tribe lay scattered. Bullets pocked the ground, and the heel marks of boots. We stepped among the broken flutes and drums, smashed skulls and calabashes. And, if in the clearing the sun was savage, we trembled with cold.

We brought the bones together for burning and, even now, they set up a dull clatter in my mind. Then we set fire to the *yano*. Everything, said Cûcla, must burn to ashes. All night I held her close to my heart. We watched the fire. It burned for two days.

The evening of the last day, Cûcla made a soup of plantain the colour of the sun. She took a handful of ash and stirred it in. As we swallowed, the spirits of her people composed themselves; they slept. Cûcla made me promise never to speak of them, or else disturb their slumber.

CHAPTER EIGHT

BUTTONS AND THE BLUE MAN

Lamprias de Bergerac

At the mouth of the Japura, four wobbly rooms sag and totter on wormy posts painted blue. This hovel has a name: the *Bem-Aventurança*, and a speciality: python steaks fried in coconut lard. The *Bem-Aventurança* can sleep fourteen on floor mats, but there are never so many travelling through that hole at the same time.

On our way to São José, we stop here for my mail and a red satin dress for Cûcla. She is delighted, but the dress – her first – doesn't do her justice. There is one short letter from Jane:

> Lamb. Your Jane's left whoring for the lights. I'm off to make my fortune with the hole in my face and not t'other one. Your loving Spider.

The innkeeper is a saggy-eyed geezer who lives with a mulata of remarkable beauty; Mea Culpa hoes the corn, raises turtles and fries the snake. Cûcla and I sit down together at one of the chipped tables and sip cup after cup of Mea Culpa's heavenly mocha. We are at once cornered by a bull-necked businessman from Syria who boasts about a bargain he has made in buttons, red string and cough syrup in São José. He plans to barter this junk with the Indians in exchange for precious furs.

In the middle of his pompous delivery, a singular man, a 'blue man' (as Cûcla called blue-eyed, raven-haired men) staggers in from the forest, looking thirsty. This man of savage and solitary life cannot be over thirty, but his flesh is so weathered it is more like saddlehide than skin. He reaches for a handful of 'little negresses', and, spilling a couple onto the counter, asks hoarsely for a bottle of gin. The Syrian walks over and prods the tiny diamonds with a filthy finger.

'Popcorn,' he sneers. Expecting trouble, the innkeeper backs off.

The Syrian, a quarrelsome sonofagun, picks up a diamond and drops it into his mouth. He clears his throat and spits – a bull's eye between Blue's boots. Blue says nothing; he just squints.

'Only a fool'd expect good gin for this crap.' He brushes the diamonds from the counter and onto the floor. 'Dog's teeth. Gizzards of buzzards.'

Blue is incredulous.

'You're crazy!' he snorts. 'And you're a nitwit. Gimme a glass,' he adds and the geezer, hunched behind his bar, pours out a drink. Stretching his arm, he passes it up to Blue.

'Nitwit? Nitwit?' The Syrian is unfamiliar with the word 'nitwit'.

'A sucker, Buttons. A boob. Fancy fur in the Amazon's as rare as fossilized shit in a brothel.' (Fossilized shit? I wonder – One of Cletis Twigger's fascinations. Had Blue and Twigger met?)

'Rare as *what*?'

'Somebody, meathead, has been pulling your leg.'

Buttons begins to shout. He says his name is (sounds like Fizzle). He says no man has ever pulled his leg.

'Somebody, Fizzle, has been telling you tales.' He speaks softly.

'This jungle is crawling with furry beasties!' the madman screams. Hadn't the skinny fairy ever heard of pumas? Jaguars? Ocelots?'

'Buttons,' said Blue, 'you've got a big mouth and you've got a big heart. Why, you're as trusting as a little baby being diapered by his nurse—'

'*Sonofabitch, I'll kill you!*'

'But we Irish fairies are clairvoyant, and I can see your naked arse clear as crystal. Fancy bringing cough syrup to people dying of syphilis. Fancy bartering buttons with people who don't even wear clothes!'

'They'll string them up! Man – they'll make fucking necklaces!'

'Leave the Indians alone. And bugger off. I've had enough of your bullshit.' And leaning over the top of the bar he hands his empty glass to the innkeeper who is still crouched on the floor.

Cûcla slides under the table just in time to miss seeing an airborne razor slice an eyebrow from the Irishman's face. He slaps his hand over the wound and his blood pisses between his fingers. Then suddenly, magically, the point of a long, tapered knife appears poised up the Syrian's nose.

'Fitzbutton,' says the wounded man evenly, taking his time, 'upon reflection I've decided to sell your skin to a Queer, an Eminent Acquaintance, a collector of Curiosities . . .' The point of his knife distends the Syrian's hairy nostril dramatically. A pearl of blood swells in the bristles of his moustache.

'. . . a venerated professor I know who's asked me to keep a look-out for Peculiarities.'

'*Drinks!*' I shout, '*Drinks on me!* Enough talk of skins,' I whisper to Blue, 'young man, you're bleeding profusely. I propose liquor, I propose an elegant meal. A proposal of *peace*, boys!' And I nod to the geezer whose prominent posterior gathers velocity. He bustles to a table with bottles of Rio de Janeiro gin, washed glasses and a dish of freshly sliced lemons. Scowling, Mea Culpa arrives with hot water and bandages. Her bosom jiggling she fixes Blue's face, quickly, expertly – as if she cared for wounds daily (and perhaps she does). Then she mops up the table – the blood, spilled water and a funny looking caterpillar which is in fact the Irishman's eyebrow. I raise my glass.

'To Brazil, where all the nations and races of men live together in harmony.' Blue astounds me by exploding into mad laughter. He doubles up, sputtering, holding his sides, nearly weeping. At last he composes himself and polishes off his gin in one sour, fiery gulp. I fill his glass.

'To suckers.' He toasts the businessman from Syria. 'To the dreams of gullible men.' I think: *They are both mad.* And quickly standing shout:

'TO OUR DREAMS!'

'To our dreams!' Buttons echoes and the eyes of that lunatic sparkle with tears.

From the open balcony I watch Cûcla walk along the riverbank in her new dress. She holds the shining skirt up to the setting sun, uncovering all her lovely little secrets. I will have to explain to her about dresses. Dresses and everything else.

Mea Culpa carries in some corn fritters and a bottle of *Menstruação*. I call Cûcla to supper.

'Forgive me, my friend,' says the Syrian, mopping his neck with his hand. 'I have a terrible temper. I pick fights when in fact I'm all alone, you see, in this godforsaken country, and looking for companionship. I wanted only to strike up conversation.'

'An unusual method . . .' Blue gives him a wry smile.

'It is my way, a custom of my country, even. First you make a man your enemy, you fight and then you make it friends.'

'In most countries,' says Blue, 'it works the other way round. Let me see that razor.'

Buttons unfolds the razor and lays it out upon the table. It is curved, a perfect crescent with a Moorish handle of tooled silver. Blue who knows his stuff whispers:

'A Boabdil. Fifteenth century.'

Buttons agrees, 'He is very, very old. His name: Head-Slicer. Sharp enough to halve a coconut. Best of all, with a little distance, he works like a *boomerong*, see?' And raising his thick arm, with a snap he throws the razor into the air. Everyone ducks. With a high, singing sound Head-Slicer orbits the room before winging back, tame as a kitten, to its master's hand.

'One slip and you kiss all fingers goodbye!' The Syrian laughs. 'Take him,' he says to Blue. 'I give him to you. In friendship. Yes, I insist and will be very vexed should you be foolish enough to refuse. I will show his working, not hard, practice – just a little trick to learn, a little trick of mind and hand and heart. You see?'

Blue, who has been holding his breath ever since the razor took off around the room, exhales. He nods, folds the razor and silently pockets it.

Mea Culpa brings freshly roasted peanuts, dumplings and Cûcla's favourite – steamed shrimp with ginger. We can hear the snake sizzling in the kitchen, and continue to drink. Soon the two men are exchanging national recipes, obscene stories, memories. Cûcla scrambles to my lap and cooing falls asleep in my arms.

Mea Culpa lights the kerosene lamps and Blue and I talk while Buttons sits quietly caressing his beard and staring, hungrily perhaps, into the abrasive surfaces of the Irishman's eyes.

I was curious about this drifter with first-rate looks, fifth-rate diamonds and a gift for gab. He spoke a fluent French, Spanish and Portuguese and he had attempted to strike up a conversation with Cûcla over supper in various Japura dialects: Who was she? Where was she from? But those ghosts were sleeping soundly, not to be disturbed, and she looked away and held to me, fighting tears. And he, looking sad, sad and somehow knowing, had not insisted. And yes, he had met Cletis Twigger, the man with the chronic cold; he had even sold him a Rampant Impossibility, a chimera stuck together with glue. He had worked for Twigger, digging up the fossil bones of *megatheria* and their coprolites in caves. But that was long ago and far away. Something about the Syrian had reminded him of Twigger . . . Buttons beamed.

'Nice company!' He nodded, not a little soused. 'A good time!'

As for the diamonds, he had picked them up scrabbling around an abandoned mine; there is plenty of gravel left, but he doesn't intend to go back for more. I ask if the mine belongs to Rosada.

Those amazing eyes are eclipsed by shadow.

'Satan walks the Amazon, and his hooves fit the prints of that man's fancy boots exactly. I'd give my soul for Rosada's life. Once he layed fifty lashes on me for giving water to a dying man. My back is like a valley ravaged by glaciers and fire.' Buttons wants to see Blue's scars but Blue only smiles ironically.

'My back's *nothing*,' he says.

'Nothing!' Buttons roars. 'Nothing much!' He slaps his knee.

Blue continues, 'I worked for Rosada. Tough work. Rubber. Covering the territory, moving from tree to tree. I'd heard stories but I needed the work and I wasn't listening to stories. I was a fool.' He is quiet. I can see him going over the memory in his mind, a memory like a corpse cradled in a ditch, considering it, stuck with it.

'Only when I saw the head of an Indian, wrapped in a

banana leaf being passed around from hand to hand, did I understand just what Rosada meant when he'd call his freaks together and say, "Let's go hunting, boys." They'd go with the army to punish the tribes that refused to be pacified; the ones who refused slavery.

'One day they brought in a young Indian, a boy barely sixteen. Rosada organized a shooting contest. It was evening; some of us were dog-tired and just hanging around. My back was still raw and I wasn't moving.

'They tied that boy eagle-spread to a tree and ever since Evil's been eating away at the back of my brain like a rat, yes, just as if my head was in a cage with a famished rat. Did I tell you he was beautiful, and smooth-limbed and strong? He clenched his teeth to keep himself from screaming. He looked like your lady, fine-featured, gentle; he could have been her brother. Maybe he was.

'The object of Rosada's game was to sacrifice parts of the boy without actually killing him. One of Rosada's thugs shot off his thumbs. He was an accomplished marksman – they all were, and he razed them clean. But that's nothing. They shot at the boy's penis next. So that Rosada could aim at the boy's balls.

'I started running. His screams followed me. Still do. I've been on the road ever since. That act is the rat I carry in my mind.'

He is quiet. The Syrian is weeping.

After a time I say, 'You asked Cûcla to talk about herself. But she can't. Her *yano* lies in ashes, and all her tribe too.'

Blue holds onto his glass with both hands. His hands are steady but his voice is shaking.

'. . . Once Rosada and his boys captured an entire tribe. Rosada put everyone to work except for the very small children. These were shot and fed to his dogs. I didn't want to believe that story when I heard it. That was when I wasn't listening to stories.'

'There were fingers missing . . .'

'Rosada's men collect them. They dry them and string them up. Just as Indians are said to do with buttons.'

The Syrian scrambles from the table, knocking over a chair in his haste. We can hear him spitting up snake over the balcony.

The following morning was one of those glorious Amazonian mornings flooded with alabaster light; the brilliant surface of the dark waters shivered as if sequins, by the hundreds of thousands, had been scattered there. The joyous sounds of birds and frogs filled the air – even the peeling *Bem-Aventurança* looked good.

Our boat rolled ever so softly on the water. Cûcla and I made sweet love to honour the day and to exorcize the sounds and smells and sights of a *yano* filled with human bones on fire. I thanked the stars she was so young and resilient.

We got off the boat to take our leave of the *Bem-Aventurança* and share a steaming pot of freshly roasted coffee and a gargantuan platter of fried bananas with our friends of the previous night. Buttons still wanted to try his luck in the jungle, if only to bring back a lizard skin and some stories. He was engaged to be married to a girl he had never seen but with pubic hair (according to his mother who had examined her attentively in the public baths) 'so thick a man could get lost in it'. The Amazonian trip was a wedding gift, the bachelor's last bash. Blue proposed to travel with him for a week or two.

'To teach the simpleton, the sucker, the stupid boob the ropes.' I expected to see another razor fly but no, this tirade was received with quiet laughter.

Clouds were humping now, coupling by the twos and threes

and fours and fives. There was a bank of them piling up behind us like mountains of snow, and an eager wind whipped across the water. We said goodbye. Mea Culpa was smiling, a dazzling sight. Buttons and the Blue Man stood on the balcony holding hands. As we picked up steam they waved.

CHAPTER NINE

PALACES OF REVENGE

Lamprias de Bergerac

The storm chasing us, we pushed on swiftly to São José. We docked in wind and rain. The Palace Caboose was shuttered and silent, Cûcla whispered: haunted. We found Laotse in the kitchen bottling oyster sauce. With great pain of heart I learned of Evangelista's murder. What was left of her body had been found tied to a tree still swarming with ants. Senhor Rosada had been seen paying gambling debts with her rings.

In panic the girls had scattered to Iquitos, to Belem, to Porto Veho, to Rio. Thin with worry and chagrin, Laotse spent his days dusting, scrubbing, planting *pei-tsei* and installing electric fans in every room. He had inherited the Palace and he dreamed of bringing it back to life. He talked of plans for a steam-bath, a marble fountain (he had never forgotten a boyhood visit to Versailles), an aviary and a gazebo. He suggested that I write to Uma and Förtjusande, my Swedish friends in Belem.

Many weeks passed before Cûcla became accustomed to living in the city. She would halt in her tracks and, with narrowed eyes and quivering nostrils, attempt to decipher an unfamiliar sound – the clatter of hooves on cobblestones, ringing churchbells, the screeching trolleys, a door-knocker slamming, a key turning in a lock, a passing bicycle, even rain against a windowpane – searching her memory for the unknown source and, when she did not find it, collapsing into tears, and, when she did, laughter.

But she loved the 'Palace Yano', its thick carpets the colour of bird's eggs and cream, the polished windows and freshly painted, milky rooms, the ornamental flourishes of its ceilings. Above all, she was enthralled by a priceless animated clock and would sit for hours at a time waiting for the tiny silver door to open with a snap. Her patience was always rewarded by the miniature embraces of an ebony man and an ivory woman.

Laotse adored Cûcla. He taught her how to use a knife and fork and to trim her nails with scissors. He explained the Mysteries of the Garter, the Laced Boot, the Buttoned Glove. He taught her to samba in high-heeled slippers. He plucked haunting melodies on the Chinese guitar and those nights when Cûcla was visited by the ghosts that must remain nameless, Laotse's guitar was the boat that sped her to sleep.

Early one morning there was a great clatter at the front door and Uma and Förtjusande had arrived, sweaty, teaty, hazel eyes and gold teeth flashing, dwarfed by their luggage: fifty cases of aquavit, the brass beds, a piano they had won playing poker and a parrot named Pops who cackled in Portuguese: 'Pay before you leave.' Laotse and the ladies were kindred spirits.

He was their *sockerdocker*, their sugar doll, their little bee, their *lillabi*. Overnight, the Palace was transformed into a cosy home where the coffee was always hot, the conversation philosophical (Laotse was a Confucian, the ladies vociferous supporters of Swedenborg), the nights festive weddings illuminated by a thousand candles and ringing to the cry of *skol*! Laotse took to making open sandwiches.

And the girls returned. Carol Cul Blanc brought with her a beauty from Trinidad with hennaed hair, a tattooed Touareg and a pair of Lithuanian twinnies who could do everything standing on their hands. The Palace's name was changed to The Palace of Revenge and a painting of my former mistress, stunning in the green dress (and commissioned by me) was hung in the parlour. I also ordered a series of paintings of all the positions of love for which the twinnies and Tombola, the Black Prince, enthusiastically posed.

We opened Carnival Week and celebrated with champagne and oysters to see the Palace humming once again with famished men who raising their voices in song pressed about a piano festive with iced whisky, *batidas*, and naked buttocks.

And there was news from Jane. She was on tour with thirty young men whose wardrobes included gossamer wings. When the curtains parted in Rio, Bahia (and later, Paris, Berlin, London, Madrid, New York and Dublin) Jane could be seen swinging on a giant tortoise-shell suspended by wire and paper vines in a jungle equipped with monkeys, toucans and a domesticated jaguar.

Jane would kick out over the orchestra, part those already famous lips and sing her *Arawak Lullabye* in a voice said to be a cordial of bitter oranges and hot chocolate – sensational! And Nadar, who, after having seen her in Paris and taken her photograph, was quoted thus in one of Angelo Mariani's publications:

> *Qu'est que c'est le paradis?*
> *D'écouter La Tarantule*
> *En se branlant le radis*
> *En buvant du Vin Mariani!*

(The third line was in fact deleted as being too obscene. These obscene lines Angelo published separately for the libraries of friends.)

The following week Cûcla and I left for Rio. I packed everything into the steamboat – Cûcla's new dresses and gifts from Uma, Förtjusande and Laotse (he had given her the wonderful clock), my books and notebooks and splint box herbariums, soil specimens, tubers and dust. I tried to convince Cûcla to give the marmoset – still unfortunately with us – to the ladies. But the creature held to Cûcla's leg with such tenacity he could not be prized off. For the first time furious with me, Cûcla intoned a low, growly *kêkêkêkêkêkêkê*!

In those days, the arrival into the port at Rio de Janeiro was always spectacular. The water, filled with billions of microscopic crustacea, shone like nowhere else in the world. Cûcla sang down to it and dolphins circled our boat barking. White blossoms hurried out to us on the wind and Cûcla caught some with her tongue.

'Soon,' I said, 'you will be catching snow.'

'*Snaouw?*'

'The stuff Uma described—'

'*Snaouw* . . .' Cûcla closed her eyes. She could not imagine it. 'Cold flowers,' Uma had said. 'When they fall at night together they grow into silent, crouching, white pumas. But when you hold one in your hand it disappears.'

'Cow frowels!' Cûcla dreamed.

We disembarked and took a room resplendent with mirrors at the Copacabana. Fresh mango was fed to the marmoset in the bathtub and, after a passionate, reconciliatory nap, Cûcla and I went down to dinner. I remember she wore a Poiret dress seeded with pearls. The hotel had been electrified since my first visit and the atmosphere was extravagant.

Cûcla's cropped hair had grown. She wore it in the fashion of the day, puffed about her face and ears like petals or nesting wings. Wild honey from the forest, her flushed skin emanated a dark perfume. I felt its beauty aching in my fingers.

Cûcla's attention was drawn to a skeletal, solitary diner with diamonds snapping at his wrists, his neck and even his ears. Frowning, he devoured a lobster with prudent concentration. Sensing that he was being watched, his lizard's eyes darted and for one interminable instant settled upon Cûcla with a singularly repugnant look of covetousness. With a shudder, she looked away.

Perhaps he was celebrating. His dessert was brought to the table flaming; it illuminated his features with an infernal blue fire. When couples nearby applauded it, he bowed his head, creating the unsettling illusion that he was responsible for the flame, the flame's choreographer.

But what was it about the scene that reminded me of Septimus my little son? That liquor burning had at once brought to mind the destruction of my Darwin, Martius and Spix, my Humboldt and Auguste de Saint-Hilaire, my Cuvier, Lamarck and Lund ... *Perhaps*, I thought, *the man is an incubus; it is he who fathered the monster, not I* ... But then my heart constricted, for the truth was so much more bitter than the fantasy.

The dining room was then suddenly plunged into darkness. Cûcla, expecting a surprise, a floor show or magic act, sucked in her breath and squeezed my arm. There was a sound, like a distant high wind; then a muffled hiccup and our eyes were drawn once more to the stranger's table where the flames had come back to life. A tower of blue fire leapt halfway to the ceiling and danced, supple as a whip, about an object I could not define. When, into the dim, eerie blue radiance, waiters came scurrying with silver candelabras illuminating the room and the object in the dish, I saw a severed head like a melon swimming in a bath of phosphorus. The body – still in its chair – was folded in two like a jack-knife. From the neck blood poured into a thickly agitated pool. And, as the drunken room veered in panic and disorder, the dead man's name orbited the air in an incessant, sinister buzz: *Rosada, Rosada; Senhor Rosada.*

I should add that the Copacabana lost no customers and

that the bellboy who invented a new drink he called the 'Flaming Death' was at once promoted to elevators. That whimsical boy was to become the hotel's General Manager. In the early 1940s I named a miniature scarlet *cymbidium* 'Boabdil', and a startling green cattleya 'Revenge'. But the most beautiful orchid of all, a bronze-tipped, tiger-striped, clove-scented *phalaenopsis*, I named – Cûcla.

CHAPTER TEN

ENEMIES AND EGG-HEADS

Septimus de Bergerac

El, the God of the Israelites, is, like P'pa, a bigamist, and his *membrum virilum*, big as a fist, engenders the Dawn and the Twilight. El is a bull with a bull's pizzle. The mass betrays the degree of profligacy.

These many, long, eventful years, P'pa has spent in North America, a continent suppurating beneath the pustular itch of racial laxity. There he froliks and magiks with his wayward rib, that savage female who worships baboons and owls and who paints her buttocks with charred grease. Only when the skies are dripping with oil, the oil of savages, of Jews and other scum parasites – impostors, charlatans, madmen, mathematicians, hypochondriacs, vampires, psychiatrists, ragpickers, journalists, intellectuals, theatricals, tinkerers, so-called *thinkers*, tailors, sneering satirists reeking of smoked herring – will Virginie be absolved of this humiliation.

Distrust men with skulls which defy classification. The Brachycephalic man is exemplarily Occidental. His skull is round, like a rubber ball, or a ball of ivory; he looks his interlocutor straight in the eye, oblique gestures are unknown to him, he is always candid, straightforward, above board. He is genial and intelligent, but – unlike the oriental – never crafty. He holds himself erect and his laughter, clear and sonorous, rebounds joyously. This elastic laugh (and I am thinking now of Kindergarten) is characteristic of the Brachycephalic Aryan; it has nothing to do with the Jew's bitter irony, the Chinaman's smirk, the Negro's bark. Distrust those who sneer.

Baldness testifies: my own head is perfectly round. And as classically Brachy as the heads of Cicero, Hadrian, Homer, Vercingetorix, Alcibiades. Napoleon had a round head as did Caesar. But Blum, Citroën, Michelin and Renault all have heads shaped like eggs. Darwin has a lump.

The longer the head, the longer the sexual part, the more doubtful the subject. Cerebral superiority is the privilege of the round-headed man, the man with a skull like a globe. The forehead's sweeping curvity indicates courage and wisdom, the firm, well-rounded chin announces sound moral judgement, substantial powers of memory and vivacity. However, a perpendicular, and, above all, *lopsided* forehead set above a long face terminating in a pointed chin is, at its best, a sign of mediocrity and, at its worst, stupidity, cupidity, curiosity. A bony, irregular forehead identifies an opinionated pretentious and quarrelsome nature.

This discussion brings me, teeth grinding, to a halt. It occurs to me that P'pa's lifetime of Manichean meddling with those wet orchids of his (a species of self-abuse – that insane hocus-pocus called *hybridization*!) is but a reflection of his own irresponsible insemination of a Chinawoman and (thank God!) sterile fornications with housemaids, whores, Jews and that imp masquerading as a woman, Cûcla – a monkey's name, the name of a puppet or a clown.

To hell with bigamists, communists, Jew tycoons, journalists with elliptical heads, agitators, homosexual spies, writers of subversive books, Italian anarchists, astronomers, arsonists . . . Ladies and Gentlemen, the Occident has a cancer, a cancer named Democracy. The Occident – too big-hearted for her own good – writhes beneath a rash of hobos, Bagel-Barons and leeches. The Occident has a tapeworm, a tapeworm named Liberalism. The Occident is being bled to death by the ghoul bats of Jewry; the sticky spermatozoa of long-dingled black

78

men, yellow men, red men contaminate the virtuous Mother Race, perhaps irretrievably.

One day they'll nail P'pa for tinkering with Mother Nature, as if she were a whore peddling cheap tricks in a room smelling of the chamberpot.

The exemplary totem of the Master Race, the round-headed race, is the globe. It signifies the moon, the aureole of saints, the Maternal Teat. Did not a shining sphere protect and guide Napoleon? The Brachy invented the spoken word and the first sound he uttered was *AM*. (Maman, Adam, Am, Amen, etc.) *AM* lies at the roots of all Indo-European languages. He invented the compass, the clock, the wheel, the all-powerful zero. He constructed Stonehenge, the Forum, the Amphitheatre. The true Brachy never leaves the well-trodden path of the Possible. I have noticed that the demonic suggestion that the ancestors of man were microscopic molluscs is demonstrative of an idea in perpendicular progression: i.e. MOLLUSC → MONKEY → MAN. Such a progression can only be the product of an egg-shaped skull; an intrinsic imbalance produces a tidal wobble in the fluids of the brain and occasions a fascination for the Peculiar, the Mystical and the Magical.

The Dolchycephalic's root syllable, *MOG* (still evident in the early Chaldean) means magician. Mog, Mogol, Molog, M'grel, Mo'b – the evolution is self explanatory. The attempt to quadrate the circle (and so corrupt it beyond recognition) is an invention of the Dolchy. What is the primary totem of the Oriental? The star. The star and the obelisk and the hideous pyramid. It was the Dolchycephalic Arabs who invented geometry. This aberrant passion for angularity has reached its paroxysm in recent history as expressed in the theoretical trash of cocaine-crazed Freud and that morbid eater of clocks, Einstein. These two jokers are without doubt the most dangerous Dolchys of any epoch. They would have us disregard Time and question Motherhood. According to the cockeyed Einstein, Space and Time are mere constructs of the mind. Next thing we know, the Americans will be making pocket-watches out of bubble-gum! (I am myself convinced that Time is composed of Wind. Wind is the generator of the electrical manifestations of Ether: lightning, thunder, rainbows, the aurora borealis. God is the motor of the World, Time's windmill, if you will.)

The primacy of Perfectly Round Things came to me early; I have already said that I was unusually precocious. At the age of eight I suffered cruelly from insomnia. Balls of fire were forever spinning across my field of vision and I suffered implacable pain in all my extremities – particularly at the tip of my prick which had been repeatedly tweaked with ferocity by P'pa's Chinese concubine. I had nightmares and had acquired the habit of throwing myself to the floor in my sleep.

These discomforts were made bearable by certain miraculous pleasures: I repeatedly found coins, round candies and marbles in my pockets – gifts from a Divine Source I was unable to identify.

One night, as I lay prostrate with pain and terror after a hellish nightmare of a dwarf Chinaman who tumbled into my bedchamber, coiled in a black cloud, and who magiked me (exciting me to abuse myself with a pencil – and what is a pencil if not an obelisk?), a little white dog flew out of my ear singing:

You will be a god. You will be God.

And I saw, shining in the mirror over my bed, my own head orbited by a circle of light. It came to me that the circle and the globe are one unto themselves and that a perfect sphere, set to spin on an immaculate plane, will spin forever; set to roll, it will roll to the end of time.

Sooner or later, a perspicacious child – as was I – will notice that the word God is the word dog spelled backwards. A heathen child will make a joke of it. I, in this simple, stunning anagram, perceived the flaming nucleus of Truth.

What began as boyish conjecture late at night alone in my chilly room (not long after I was banished from M'man's creamy teats), developed over the years into what was to become my celebrated 'Thunder And The Primary Totemic Symbols'. I was but seven years old when I came to the conclusion that mankind's primal totemic Godhead is the D O G (the dogged God: the Unyielding) or the L I O N – both have the same emblematic signification – with a G L O B E tucked beneath his paw. It symbolizes, with force and economy, the superiority of the White Race, its intrinsic control over all things cosmic and worldly. Philistines and physicists may say that the world is not round, that it bulges at the poles and that the Universe is shaped like an egg. But even a beardless Brachy's common sense tells him that the Universe is perfectly round, a luciferous globe poised upon the Ether of Eternity. For it is evident, is it not, that an egg-shaped universe would – sooner or later – topple over and crack open. (Or it would sink.)

Who can escape the circle? P'pa tried. Fool that he was, he believed in Perpendicularity and Progress. That capricious copulator followed his cock, thinking it was leading him towards the Truth. But the earth is round; the first step away from Start is the first step towards Finish. Your Destiny, P'pa, is a game of goose!

At the beginning of the century, P'pa went to America and left us forever. M'man took the case to court, where he lost all his feathers. But ever the prestidigitator, he made off with enough to buy himself and his dancing ape the Kropotkin Estate, forty acres of Rusky eccentricity: boxwood mazes, rose-gardens and thickets, a manor house of stucco that sprawls along the banks of the Hudson River like a crazy Youssouf's movie set. The estate includes a greenhouse (Kropotkin insisted on fresh, ripe strawberries in his corn-flakes each and every morning of the year) designed by a fantastical fairy Spaniard whose name eludes me (Goya? Goody? Gatsby?) who found inspiration for the roof by stuffing his winter underwear with grapefruit and dipping it into plaster before hanging it up to dry. I was just a fledgling demi-orphan when P'pa bought this stinking *sanctum sanctorum*. He has since constructed six more glass houses and packed them to overspill with the negro voodoo of his unbalanced mind. It makes me furious to think of that immensity of malignity, those scrofulous abortions P'pa calls his Transcendent Species. Transcendent, my arse! I saw P'pa not long ago on the cover of *Time*. *Time* called him the 'Einstein of Biology'. P'pa, in the eyes of the world, a Jew! The biggest Jew of all, and I am about to cook his goose!

And she? And she? The animal? She runs around naked as a goldfish, shits in the roots of the *ornithowhatsitall*, mossy-skinned and webby after a lifetime of hanging around in an artificial rainstorm, singing her odd, primitive melodies to an ocean parcelled out in test-tubes. In other words, making a fool of herself. (And an even bigger fool out of that fornicator, P'pa – by putting horns as thick as bananas on his tarred and feathered head again and again and again!)

Enough talk of P'pa, for the time being. I, too, have been busy. And, if the state of my gums proves to the contrary, my life has not been spent in teeth-gnashing alone. I like to think of myself as a man of action, of indirect action; not your infantryman, mind you, but more your theoretician. The infantry takes its orders from the man with the brain. I have that brain and have put it to good use.

I was educated by the Jesuits and we hit it off famously. Later, I went to the University of Poitiers where I earned my doctorate with honours in linguistics. (I studied under the notorious Stormkraps.) And, when Headache, Hernia and Hemialgia kept me, *hélas*, from serving Mother France (my dream was to become an officer in the Foreign Legion and to do my duty in the colonies), I decided to become Brachycephalic Spokesman Par Excellence: an Influence and an Inspiration. A catalyst. In every book, speech, letter and pamphlet; in every editorial (I have written monthly for *The Public Good* since 1918) the Wind of Promise like a phoenix hung above the horizon.

After True Man was decapitated (and his head was round. It didn't fit anywhere but beneath the knife. True Man, like P'pa's tricky *paphiowhoosis*, was an aberrance to the end), M'man had the house done over from top to bottom and, in the process, uncovered P'pa's adolescent love letters from the Jewess Marta Strada – a thick wad of filthy spunk! Strada was just the sort of individual who would rally to de Gaulle. Jewish trollops and fishermen – the Resistance smelled of rotten fish. After her arrest, someone, some cretin, some driveller, suggested that Strada, then in her nineties, was innocent. You know the joke? The one about the Jewess who inherits a fortune from her grandfather Moses Grossnozzel? As beautiful as Venus, as rich as Croesus and as innocent as Dreyfus. Innocence! My arse!

CHAPTER ELEVEN

TREASURE OF TREASURES

Lamprias de Bergerac

Once, long ago, kings were wizards. The King-Wizard was named Sire and to work enchantment he stood in the centre of a pentacle – his magic circle: Sire in O. In the manuscript Savinien left behind, he wrote his name thus:

SIRANO

Savinien wrote: 'The circle of enchantment is drawn in sand.' He also wrote, 'The practice of Alchemy is a ladder of sand.' And: 'I take my pleasure in the elusive embrace of the Mystery.' Of Savinien, it was said: 'He wore life like a ceremonial garment . . . He was always dreaming.'

Savinien kept scraps of tadpole's tail alive for three days in 'mercurial dew', the recipe for which has been unfortunately lost. He gazed upon his phials of glass, in which the cloudy constellations of living tissue slowly drowned, and he dreamed of producing a frog from a fragment of its own tail.

Savinien ejaculated into his mysterious soup and filled twelve phials with the new mixture. He sealed them and imagined the little children who he hoped would one day appear, their hands and faces pressed eagerly against the glass. He called them: 'My little lions of jelly', and 'my little star-squids'. But sperm and the milk of birds produced something so indescribably foul that he threw everything into the fire.

Savinien concocted a new environment: mineral, philosophical and noble. It contained potable gold, the oil of talc, ignited artifices and the powders of projection. Into it he slipped some very fine slices of the roots of radishes. The cells died. To the dissolved minerals he added yeast and sugar. Intuition and hazard had now created a microcosm, the Humid Star of Alchemy. Before they died, the cells multiplied.

Savinien dreamed of runes, of ciphers floating in his chalices, his precious phials of glass: soundless, touchless, formless, imperishable. He dreamed of an infinity of perfect cells imbedded in a magic, life-giving jelly, like planets impearled in time. And Savinien imagined the universal library of all things. It comprehended the treasures of the cosmos in sealed glass phials, pulsating like wings or like thought. Each phial contained the mercurial dew and one living cell. Each living thing – radish, frog, lion, human-being – was kept suspended, dynamic and eternal: seed syllables, the unuttered words of God. A jungle's worth of monkeys, an ocean of whales could be carried as reduced models from earth to other worlds. (Savinien also invented the space-ship.)

Savinien imagined the oceans of the dark side of the moon filled with the scintillating monsters of the earth's deep: eels and eyeless fish; the jewelled continents of the sun seeded with pumas; Venus and Mars – orchid isles.

Savinien likened the philosopher's stone to the egg of the peacock which contains the promise of a multitude of functions and forms and colours. He believed that a cell from any living thing has the intrinsic power to retrace the steps of its history back to the very beginning and become an embryo. He died before he found the answer, but he knew that the answer was there.

Like a planet, a vegetable cell has two poles. One will give birth to a root and one to a stem. But an isolated cell loses its polarity; it can develop in any direction. And if – as it floats within a suitably nutritive environment – it is rotated, its polarity is momentarily suspended. The cell will produce neither root nor stem, but instead exact copies of itself:

CESTE PIERRE EST VEGETALE

In 1903, Cûcla and I sailed for France. Angelo had generously offered me a small greenhouse and laboratory space. Upon my request he rented for us a charming place just up the street.

Angelo was as intrigued as I by the notion that the cells might be rotated and he wanted to be near when I undertook the experiments. I unpacked my dust and tubers and got down to work at once. From the laboratory windows I could see Cûcla, in candystriped silk, walking arm in arm with her tutor and companion, the bubbly Mademoiselle de Babel, 'Babe'; the marmoset scampering along after the ladies' skirts.

O beautiful moment! Paris was innocent then, innocent of the horror to come. O beautiful women of Paris, as innocent as the creatures of Paradise. The Parisiennes (and Cûcla among them) were cat and bird together, catbirds, dripping with jewels and fluffy with feathers. Paris purred; everything evoked Eros – from the entrance to the métro to Angelo's collection of Gallée glass. All the women of the world were in Paris then. Is it surprising that we met up with Tarantula Jane?

The Spider was known in Paris as *L'Amazone*. Lovelier than La Belle Otero, she could kick as high as La Goulue; discussion around the cluttered tables of the cafés was hot: who was the greater actress? *L'Amazone* or the dazzling Jewess, Sarah? Rumours circulated that the two were lovers, but at dinner *chez* Mariani, Jane told us all with a mischievous grin:

'It's because we recently shared a bath of ass's milk and a number of gentlemen present chose to pretend we were fountains at Vichy and the milk a miracle cure for impotency.'

L'Amazone was so inflammable 'the stage must be watered

down after each performance else it smoulder into cinder and ashes'. Theatre-goers who visited Gustave Moreau's exhibition of paintings and prints could not help but see Jane's face in every sphynx; was it true that she was one-third Irish, one-third Bantu and two-thirds *Catalane*? Someone said, and I think it was Colette, that 'If most of us are made of water, *L'Amazone* is made of *eau de vie*.'

All our lives we would recall with ravishment those few, short years spent at Neuilly – the steamy warmth of the Palm House in winter where Cûcla talked to the leaves, 'Doing them a world of good,' said Angelo; my first successful experiments, Babe's substantial, jolly presence (for which we could all thank Cûcla's seemingly effortless mastery of French); our first experiences of that miracle, the infant cinema (one of Angelo's many infectious passions): Méliès' *Voyage dans la lune*, his hand-coloured *La Fée libellule* in which the fairy, cradled in her fantasmagorical Amazonia, looked just like Cûcla. Cûcla, who was also picking up a little German, called the fairy 'My little *Doppelgänger*'.

Fascinating people came to Neuilly to enjoy Angelo's hospitable table and visit his coca plantations: Caruso, Colette, Sarah, La Belle Otéro, Maeterlinck, Kipling, Poincaré and the youthful Alphonso XIII who fell head over heels in love. The melancholy which ensued after Cûcla rejected him lasted, it has been said, for a lifetime and explains, in part, his reckless behaviour in motorcars.

One who became a close and dear friend was the aeronaut Louis Capazza. Handsome, audacious and a captivating raconteur he was also the creator of the silk parachute which he had himself successfully demonstrated on numerous occasions. So intrigued was Cûcla by his spectacular invention, Capazza proposed she give it a try. And so Cûcla, dressed in red harem pantaloons, her hair in pigtails, her eyes flashing comets of elation, leapt from Capazza's balloon at one thousand metres, at two p.m. the twenty-third of July – the first woman in the history of the world to use a parachute.

Babe, the King of Spain, Angelo and I, perched like bereaved volatiles on the slate roof of a cow barn, cheered with an enthusiasm that verged on hysterics (never have I ever been so terrified!) when Cûcla, howling with laughter, landed as gently as dandelion fluff in a gold field of summer wheat somewhere near Chartres.

This time of pleasure did not last for very long. Virginie's constant harassment precipitated exile. She once put Septimus – then sixteen – on the train for Paris with a brick and the request that he throw it at me (which he did), smashing a laboratory window, my spectacles and a microscope. Nabbed by Babe he did not struggle but stood his ground defiantly. I was distressed when I saw him and realized who he was. Wiping the blood from my eye I offered him lunch and a friendly talk. I told him that his poor manners reminded me of someone I had met in the Amazon – an Arab named Buttons ... I'd hoped to hook him with a tale, but he would have none of me and so was sent packing with the few francs Virginie had neglected to give him for his return ticket to Angers. As I recall, he was to all appearances particularly enraged that he had reminded me of an Arab.

After a succession of excruciating trials instigated by Virginie (and I lost them all), Cûcla and I booked passage on the *Mauretania*. In the late fall of 1908, we crossed the Atlantic at an exhilarating twenty-five knots and for three weeks the world smelled fiercely of fish and grit and salt and oil. I remember we saw the coast of America in the very early morning. Had we left the oceans of Earth for the cities of Neptune? I thought: If only Savinien could see this! Soaring in the plum-coloured haze of near winter, New York City appeared to us shivering in the water like spangled, ice-bound pyramids. When we disembarked, Cûcla clung to me expecting to see a giant at every window, a genie in every lamp. (She still thinks that like diamonds and sapphires the city regenerates itself spontaneously and silently in the heart of night.)

Before the move upstate, we spent two weeks at the Metropolitan Hotel, giddy among too many padded rockingchairs, pickpockets, hotel detectives, revolving doors and bellboys. Once I had ordered the glass I needed for my work and Cûcla had made numerous trips to Lord and Taylor's, we visited the city, grave and gay together, as curious as cats. (That first week we ate liverwurst *and* Welsh rarebit at the same meal and survived.) Then burdened with crates of dishes, of glass bottles, tubes and corks, my library and other things too numerous to name, we took the train to Barrytown and there, having hired two carriages and an empty milk delivery truck, trundled ourselves off to the Yano Kropotkin.

A white gravel driveway winding for near a mile past oaks and startled foxes, slate roof reflecting in the sky. Four chimneys, eleven flues, a shameless display of gingerbread. The decorative brickwork of the façade far prettier than in the photograph. A profusion of white framed windows and garden walls festooned with stucco pomegranates. Sunlight skidding on the pink and white marble of the entrance – an entrance even Laotse, with all his imagination for luxury, could not have dreamed up for the Palace of Revenge. French doors framing a prodigious view of the Hudson River, the Catskill Foothills, a bay and woodlands. A doe gazed out at us from the boxed hedges' mind-boggling geometries. And within that stunning solar ship – Kropotkin's greenhouse – at each turning, the blessings of Apollo.

Kropotkin had left us his wicker lawn furniture; we found

it wintering on the veranda. (It still sits on the lawn in the shade, just as it did our first summer – forty-five years ago! Though now all the seats sag.) He also left a cut velvet sofa – its erotic possibilities revealed to us that first evening before a boisterous fire fed with splintered packing crates and straw.

Evangelista's clock struck the early hours of the morning. I folded Cûcla against my heart. We made love, and Bliss, seizing us in her incandescent fist, brought Time to a standstill. The figures of ebony and ivory quieted in their little cabinet, we slept. (They have punctuated the hours of our lives with their embraces and our hunger, throughout the years, has been as constant as their own.)

Winter. I can still see Cûcla that first morning dressed to the gills in an oversize lynx jacket and rubber boots kicking up snow, growling, exhilarated and abashed. She had seen flurries in Paris, but never anything like this. White pumas crouching, yes, and also fossilized torrents of salt, forests of milk and forests of foam.

Summer. I need only close my eyes for Cûcla to appear in a negligee that washes down from her shoulders like a fall of water. She gazes dreamy, chin on fist, out of an open window at the Hudson River's meticulous morning celebrations. My memories are like that window, open to the river, open to the seasons.

Autumn. The sweet, golden light of evening, thick as syrup, and Cûcla running home from the woods past oak trees blazing scarlet.

Spring. The smell of her cornbread baking, her bluewhite crockery and potted avocados posing in all the windows. Cûcla enthralled by the sun's reflection in puddles after a thunderstorm.

Summer again. Her kitchen sink filled with soaking shells

plucked from the toiling surf of the Jersey shore. Cûcla, my flower of flesh, blooming.

At the Kropotkin Estate, beneath the muted bubbles of glass, I was able at last to grow the precious species from the seeds I had gathered in the feverish years of my exploration, and to create the hybrids of my fancy; then isolate cells and develop the nutritious cultures for them, producing *in vitro* and by the hundreds of thousands: Treasure of Treasures, Magician and King, Sirano, A Door in Sand, Spider's Furnace, The Wheel of Fortune, Perfumed Glove, Revenge, Ceremony and Cûcla. Blossoms so fabulous (and please don't think me vain, for I never think of them as *mine*, but as belonging to God, to Savinien and to Chance) they are said to be puissant aphrodisiacs. And it is true that at my first open-house exhibition: 'DE BERGERAC MERI-CLONES: FLOWERS YOU NEVER DARED DREAM', foreign celebrities, politicians, reporters, horticulturists and movie stars all landed up coupling in the Barrytown Hotel's cosy beds. Was it the combined smells of ginger and praline, patchouli, sandal and honeysuckle, or the fullblown blossoms' impudent display of tiger-striped, peachvelvety, sticky and incandescent genitalia?

Treasure of Treasures, a crossing of two of my own hybrids – Temple Fountain and Sirano – won the day. Treasure has the translucence of fine Song, high-fired porcelain and the colour of a K'ai fong *Ju* glaze. The blossom is enormous – twenty-eight centimetres across – and the perfume is indescribable, the firelight effervescence of Cûcla's ardour. It has been fabulously successful – an embarrassment really. These days no official function – wedding, coronation, inauguration, boat-launching and so on – is considered complete without her. The *Saturday Evening Post* quotes Marcel Duchamp:

'To look at Treasure of Treasures is to look into the luminous face of Desire.' Joan Crawford recently was photographed in a white Daimler blanketed with them; Cûcla showed me a sinister photograph of Liberace's swimming pool transformed into a piano-shaped vase; it is whispered that Ava Gardner sleeps on a pillow filled each night with the precious petals and that Salvador Dali eats them in salads, although this is unlikely.

Fame has led me ever more inwards, into myself and my work. I am old, a very old man and wary of so public a praise of magic. I fear I have thoughtlessly turned Mystery out into the streets, like a heartless father a wayward daughter. Treasure has become a streetwalker; anyone who can pay her price can have her. At the weddings of emirs she is scattered on the ground like common rice.

And yet . . . Treasure of Treasures was intended to be, like my Cûcla, cherished. To be prized. When her cipher's thousand twin sisters swim in their little temples of glass, the greenhouse is itself a temple, a Sun Temple flooded with light, that, filtered through a thin membrane of Spanish white, has all the translucence of inter-cellular space.

The thousands of phials appear infinite to my failing sight; the horizon fades out on all sides and I stand in the centre of a sea of possibility, my heart leaping with a breathtaking inkling of just what the Universe might be. I have dreamed that the cosmos is an endless arrangement of glass phials set row upon row like honey in the hive, each containing *pneuma*, the vital breath, the spirit of Apollo and Neptune combined.

I had another dream. It was evening and I was strolling down the aisles of the nursery, gazing upon the tender plantlets. They each had forked roots, like mandrakes, and heads. I had created little men, the alchemist's homunculus. I looked into their faces and saw the sneering mug – of Senator McCarthy! As it turned out, this dream was premonitory. Now that my colleagues talk of duplicating men, I shudder and wonder if it would not have been better to have left Mystery alone altogether; to have left her squirrelled away in the secret recesses of God's mind.

Now I have come upon a memory of a thing that, though it happened long ago, rends my heart. This shard of memory is sharp and dark.

A wide staircase of pink and green marble swept from the second storey down into the front hall. Here, on this splendid staircase, Cûcla – who had the habit of skipping barefoot up and down – tripped and fell. That night the near-infant, kicked from its nest by the violent shock, spilled from her bruised womb in webs and ropes of what looked like bloody silk.

For days Cûcla's tears streamed down her gentle face. She knew in her heart what the doctor was soon to tell us: she would never carry another child.

For a time the terror of the *yano* returned to haunt her. Perhaps because she was a woman now, no more a child; perhaps, too, because the myths and beliefs of her homeland no longer satisfied her mind and her heart, she saw a rift between Life and Death, an obscene yawning. Boa's perfect orbit had been broken. His emerald tail had slipped from his ruby mouth.

In time she found others to care for, creatures who – like our dead daughter – had been dropped unfinished into the world.

CHAPTER TWELVE

ON BEAUTY

Septimus de Bergerac

Virginie Grenier de Fourtou de Bergerac taught me all I know about Beauty; when one is unfortunate enough to have been born ugly, Beauty is a lesson that must be learned. As if to mock me, there was that sleek-limbed, broad-shouldered True Man to be contended with daily. (I swear there is always a Chinaman or a Jew jeering in a corner!)

In the nursery there hung a tall, gilded mirror, framed with cherubs and garlands of roses. Once True Man and I undressed and stood together facing it. Chubby, spotty, dwarfed beside him, I barely reached his chest and the blow to my eight-year-old pride was considerable. In my blindness, the blindness of my innocence, I saw that he was perfect. Fighting tears I hastily pulled on my clothes and ran to my M'man.

'Why am I so ugly?' I sobbed. 'And why is True Man so beautiful?'

'True Man is Chinese.' She said this with authority. 'He cannot possibly be beautiful.'

'Beauty,' she continued as she stroked my hair, 'pleases the beholder. It pleases me to behold you, my little Septimus, proof enough that you are beautiful. Beauty,' she added, 'can be found only among the well-born and the well-bred.'

With these few words she imparted to my physical self a consistency which, until then, had been sorely wanting. The ill-fitting bolts and screws of my stubby frame slipped into place. Thanks to my M'man, that day I stood taller.

How I adored my Sundays with M'man, especially those rainy

Sundays when we would sit together on her big bed playing the game called Stanley. This was a kind of chess I had read about in *The World of Youth*. I had made the board myself. For the pieces we used twenty-four spools of black cotton thread and one white spool. This was Stanley. The object of the game was for Stanley to capture all the black spools or be captured by them. We always cheated so that Stanley never lost. I was very attached to Stanley and contrived for him a paper hat so that he looked like a tiny man, robust and prosperous in his white silk suit.

According to my *Géographie*, the Hottentots of South Africa were the ugliest people on earth. There were plenty of Hottentots then. Some things disappear: Hottentots, dodoes, the Indians of Tierra del Fuego (who, according to the *The World of Youth*, were hideous).

'Beauty,' said M'man, 'is always reasonable. Beauty never goes against the grain of Mother Nature. Beauty is never excessive.'

However, there are women crazy for peculiarities and savageries. When M'man threw True Man out, he caused unimaginable havoc among the wives of our neighbours. Monsecret is one of Angers' finest streets and these were the wives of doctors, lawyers, and professors at the Catholic University! All of them pretended to feel sorry for the sixteen-year-old orphan. In fact they lusted for True Man's outsize brass knocker. I had fantasies of these women hanging like monkeys from trees; not by their tails but their necks. I wrote to their husbands to inform them of their scandalous behaviour.

Even if one has not been humiliated by the so-called fair sex time and time again, as have I, it is obvious – just look at them! – that women cannot be trusted. The haughty rotation of the pelvis (Dr Roux says: 'The sun is one of the Satans of the Universe ... Women are little ambulant suns and their pelvis is a cesspool'); the coy tossing of the head, the suggestive sideways glances and the laughter – above all the laughter.

I am willing to give credit to the inferior races for the way they handle their women. The infibulation of Negresses, Arabian wives and daughters incarcerated in kitchens, the binding of Chinawomen's feet. I like to imagine a brothel where the women – and each and every one has her feet bound – are infibulated when not in use and tied to their beds. That's *my* idea of Paradise.

This digression has touched upon the Arabs. I myself have always envied their deserts. When I grew bored attempting to imagine P'pa's peregrinations in Brazil, I admired the map of North Africa and its quiet expanses of emptiness. It came to me then, that, should the sun ever get hot enough, all the world's deserts would become glass. The earth's crust would melt, making some sort of a glaze, brilliant and brittle, and the seas would be transformed into crusts of salt thousands of square miles wide. Rendered uninhabitable, the Mother race might look upon the world from the moon, let's say, or a construction of metal in the sky, and be inspired by such perfection.

True Man was executed on a Friday morning in August, 1899. M'man and I, incognito, had rented a room with an unobstructed view of the prison courtyard. It was a poor, comfortless room and the two chairs set by the open window were of mean, unvarnished wood. Fortunately, I had thought to bring M'man's cushion.

'I hope,' she whispered, 'that the executioner will not forget to cut off True Man's shirt collar. I hate a snag; I like a job well done.'

The room's hideous proprietress, doubtless impressed by

M'man's elegant *ensemble* and my own air of precocious self-sufficiency, brought us both a small glass of rum. Although the glasses were grimy and the dark sky sweltering, we toasted in the shadows to True Man's end and a problem so neatly solved without either of us having lifted a finger.

'I knew,' said M'man, 'it would come to this. Be attentive, Septimus, all your life, to the signs and warnings of our Saviour, Jesus Christ.' This led us into an animated conversation about robbers, knaves, pickpockets, thieves and highwaymen.

'The robber,' M'man explained, 'is a sneak; he steals obliquely. The knave steals with art and the pickpocket with legerdemain. Highwaymen and thieves are no better than brutes. The robber fears discovery, the knave notoriety, the sneak to be slapped—'

Just then the first rays of the rising sun smote the elephantine blade that hung suspended in the gloom.

'That blade,' I said, 'weighs exactly sixty kilos.' M'man gasped – not with fear nor displeasure. Dust gone, the annihilation of True Man would liberate her mind, once and for all, of its cumbersome baggage.

Beneath us, the tattery crowd – the press, vampiric females, beggars and brutes, a flower-girl with a décolletage whose few secrets were frankly revealed to my bird's-eye view – stirred when the sky, as befitting the hour, churned bloody. True Man, his wrists and ankles tightly tied, appeared dragged by two prison guards and trailed by a priest. He was shirtless and his smooth, rippling chest gleamed like polished gold in the dawning light. His raven hair, and delicate, flared nostrils, the sculpted lip (and True Man had the mouth of a Khmer effigy) all kindled in my heart a paroxysm of revulsion, of anger, of envy – yes! For I could not help but remember the countless scented love-notes that fell like the petals of camellias from the letter-box to the floor and all for him, the lice-ridden, panting, sperm-stained scoundrel who spent his summer afternoons in the beds of unscrupulous bourgeoises, in ditches in the arms of seamstresses, in the dim cheese-cellars of languorous groceresses (and among the women in the milling crowd I believe I may have recognized the wife of a Député!).

This is it, I exulted, pinching myself so as not to miss a split second. In a minute, at the most two, the Chinaman will be snuffed out like a candle. Ancient history. Pass over. Kaput. No more kisses you horny scrap of animated fat! No more carousing, no more scented letters. Pitchforks and flames and a bellyful of earth. From mudhole to mudhole he clammered his innocence. But Dust's cane was smeared with the fingerprints of a short lifetime. And, anyway, a Chinaman is born guilty.

The little flower-girl, a dim-witted thing, her breasts like greasy peaches in the dusty basket of her bodice, her slattern's blood moved by my half-brother's half-naked body, threw him a pansy. And then, damn him and damn his eyes, True Man, with the look of a crazed tiger, turned his head towards the window of our little room and I swear he savaged me, savaged me with a look of unfettered ferocity and – what is worse – irony. What troubled me the most at the time was that he knew where to find me; undoubtedly, the room had a certain celebrity.

Spilling what was left of her rum onto my lap, M'man crossed herself as True Man was picked up by the seat of his pants and thrown onto the machine. She said, '*Fatale bascule!*'

An instant later, with the sound of a thunderclap, *VLAM!* and the gurgling mouth of Charybdis, True Man's head was severed from his body; a severed head is forever. Thank God he didn't weep; I cannot abide weeping.

I paid through my nose to keep the head; as pale as ivory,

the eyes open, the teeth clenched, it was brought to us wrapped in his shirt. M'man said:

'Today's flesh; tomorrow's clay.' I carried the basket.

When I graduated from the University the entire first floor of the house was painted a military green and furnished for my own private use. The couches and chairs are all a virile mahogany upholstered in the skins of dead tigers. I believe that I may be the only man alive to have camel-hide carpeting wall to wall. True Man's enigmatic skull decorates my desk; its beauty is startling and stimulates reflection. It sits in a dish of fine Moroccan brass. Also on my desk is an *aperçu* of my photography collection: a signed photograph of Pétain standing beside Xavier Vallat, of Pétain and Hitler shaking hands, of Virginie Grenier de Fourtou dressed in tulle.

From my open windows I admire three flourishing palm trees. Palms grow well in the Loire Valley and look handsome if somewhat stunted. They are sterile and bear no fruit. I have a fine oil-painting above the mantel: Touareg bedouins sitting before their tent; and above the sofa (from the arabic, *soffa*) a portrait of an albino dromedary. A pity I was not fit for service. My de Bergerac barrel-chest concealed beneath a *burnoose*, I could have cut quite a figure seated on a camel. I see us, camel and me, standing alone on a high plateau above Oran, or leading a caravan through the Sahara towards the Sudan, down past the oases of Laghouat, Ghardaia, Ouargla, El Goléa, Touat, Araouan to Timbuktu, my flesh purified by the burning sirocco. But enough wishful thinking. It is all I can do these days thump-thumping about on canes. A pause now for my pills. (I suppose I'll never know who was the first to infect my poor, pinched foreskin with the dread disease: a Jewess? A Gypsy? Could it have been a Jesuit?)

During the transformations, Dust's ancient quarters were

ripped from the house and a large, high-ceilinged room was made available for political meetings. My involvement with *Realpolitik* started off innocently enough. I was not yet twenty when I wrote a letter to *The Public Good* in answer to an article they had published:

> ... They say that Youth is brutal, disorganized, self-satisfied, egotistical, unconscious and impolite. Youth is all these things. And more. Youth is audacious, courageous, ambitious. Ah! If only Youth had a leader! All we need is to be led!
> GIVE US . . . A LEADER!

The editors were impressed and wrote to me asking for a series of articles. I first demonstrated the Rothschilds' responsibility for Napoleon's defeat at Waterloo, assuring myself from the start an enthusiastic readership. And so my professional life began. As luck would have it, the First World War broke out and it was I who wrote the biographies of Archduke Ferdinand and the spook who had killed him. These pieces glittered with orientalia – mosques and brocade and bloody rituals – which, if they had great appeal at the time, have, I admit, tarnished like cheap jewellery with age. Live and Learn! I have been writing for *The Public Good* now for almost thirty years. I cannot tell you how satisfying it is to see all those words bear fruit.

The brushfires of our Victory really gathered momentum in the thirties; the end of that decade saw the triumph of three great men: Hitler, Mussolini and Franco. The economic crises, the strikes, the scandals, the Spanish Civil War and, in its wake, the scummy flood of radical refugees whom that ragseller Blum received with open arms, his socialist government's criminal devaluation of the franc and, above all, the examples of Italy and Germany – their government's unstinting use of the mop, the broom, the paddle, the noose, the prison-cell and the gun – swelled the membership of opposition organizations and my own heart with optimism!

By 1936, Friends for Racial Purity, The Anti-Semitic League, Friends Against Foreigners and the Friends For Fascism all joined forces. We called ourselves Friends In Truth (FIT). 1936 was also the year that Blum – and he deserves to be shot in the back – had given the working classes paid vacations. *Paid vacations!* Thanks to that coddled Yid, it is impossible to visit the seaside and not be provoked by the working class, its brats and tents and garbage. And, as if paid vacations were not enough, Blum raised their salaries. The working class doesn't even walk to work any more. The bastards all have bicycles!

The fourteenth of July, 1936, when the socialist masses – Zionists, internationalists, the makers of raincoats and gloves, Algerian Jews – marched with their fists in the air, FIT was there giving them the finger and the fascist salute. According to the socialist press, we created a 'small incident'. But now, just a few years later, they are the 'small incident', the diminishing incident and we, WE GROW ALL THE TIME!

Just south of Angers stands an old tyre factory. In 1939 the place was used as a camp for the Spanish refugees; it was they who put up the fences. When in that same year the law was passed denying legal rights to nomads, electrified barbed wire was added and the Spanish ordure was forced to share the camp with Gypsies. Then (and I add with pride, thanks to me) the law was extended to include *all* wanderers – hobos, puppeteers, laundresses, bookmakers, travelling salesmen, journeymen, waffle-vendors, scissor-sharpeners, homeless drunks – all those at the bottom of life's ladder: the impure, the constipated, the choleric; madmen carrying knives or pitchforks, or bottles of acid, or socialistic propaganda (and the list is longer). We bring Jews here. This is where we brought P'pa's 'first love', that slut, that scribbler of filth: Marta Strada.

M. Xavier Vallat
Commissaire Général aux
Questions Juives, VICHY

April 19th, 1941

Esteemed Commissary General,

A Catholic and a Patriot, a militant member of *Action Française*, the *League Antisémitique de France* and a founding member of *Friends In Truth*, and knowing you to be a man of inflexible, undeviate honour, I am convinced of my duty to inform you of the subversive activities of the Jewess Marta Strada, a female known to have the morals of an open sewer and the political affiliations of a sow. She possesses a quantity of anti-Nationalist-Socialist propaganda which she distributes among the young, and in public houses vomits her Gaullist bile and Israelite's hatred of all that is just and true. I myself have seen her luxuriating in the expensive motorcar of another yid (as his name indicates): Osiris Cahen, a pimp and a reptile who shamelessly bleeds foolish but more honourable goyim by selling muskrat as mink and glass as precious stones, and who keeps his socks up with the silk garters of his whore.

I have unquestioning confidence in your authority and the manner in which you will see fit to deal with these subversive elements. At this troubled epoch, Marta Strada and Osiris Cahen are not so much a public nuisance as a public danger.

Please accept, honoured Sir, the expression of my most distinguished sentiments.

Vive Pétain!

*Septimus
de Bergerac*

CHAPTER THIRTEEN

IGNATZ AND KRAZY KAT

Lamprias de Bergerac

Cûcla, whose French was admirable, was now faced with English. She was gifted and soon fluent in a manner all her own, her conversation spiced with slang and zany, exclamatory banter she had picked up from the Sunday morning funny papers. She felt that the chatter of cats, cows, ducks, rascals and mice filled tragic gaps. Without the beeps! and wows! and moos and honks, English was no better than a mouth full of missing teeth.

That first winter in Barrytown, Cûcla, twenty but looking fifteen, received a thick envelope of Krazy Kat funnies from our nearest neighbour, Mr Tufts. *Ah the futile Foof and Fuff of it*, Krazy moans, *Oh! The Waste of Warp, a wanton wear of weft and woof!* How adequately this expressed how Cûcla felt about my trials and tribulations with Virginie, the labyrinthine bustle of New York City, the letters we found in the mail from Septimus whose life-long fixation had flowered. These venomous, often terrifying letters came every month like clockwork for over forty years. My theory is that Septimus wrote them on nights of full moon. They seethed and sputtered with the most disquieting sexual fantasies concerning Cûcla. I stopped reading them and stuffed them into boxes up in the attic.

Cûcla said, 'You should read them, lamb. He's your kid, even if he is bonkers.' But this I could not do. They were just too horrible. And I did not tell Cûcla that they were all about her, the most scandalous lies ... But now I ask myself, if I had read them, if I had had the courage, perhaps I could have saved the lives of Marta and Jane.

Other letters came, heartening and full of verve and the love of life. The Spider was still stepping high, and if a brilliant escort, a tattooed acrobat named Max, had left her for 'a floozy, a trollop named Soozie', she was making whoopie with Raoul, 'an Argentinian crooner with a dick like a schooner. The man is hot lava,' wrote Jane. 'He shits solid gold bricks.'

There was also the occasional brick from Virginie: 'To remind you that you have transgressed God's Holy Law and outraged His Majesty.'

Indo-European languages Cûcla called crusty; languages without twitters, grunts and howls could not capture and create worlds. Dry as the farts of crickets and the barks of toads. My rowdy Cûcla expressed her joy by leaping across the lawn and squealing like a maiden baboon.

The forest that flanks the Kropotkin Estate is a national park. The owls that breed there are a protected species. They are small, copper-coloured creatures who feed upon moths and mice. They are very rare, perhaps condemned, and the public is not allowed to bungle up their precarious lives. This explains the TRESPASSERS WILL BE PROSECUTED signs everywhere and why Cûcla got into hot water.

'Honestly, Offissa,' Cûcla explained to Judge Schuyler at the Rhinebeck courthouse, 'I didn't see the boy.'

'Maam, that you did not see the boy is not the offence. He saw you. In New York State it is against the law to trespass in the nude.'

'Who could take offence at my little nipples, Offissa?'

Judge Schuyler rubbed his eyes and yawned. His life was a continuous twilight cocktail hour. His pitcher of ice-water spruced up with sliced limes was spiked with gin; his lunch consisted of three Bloody Marys and a salami sandwich.

'These are not my laws, maam,' he mumbled sleepily, 'but the laws of New York State. The owls in that forest are an endangered species.'

'So, Offissa, am I.'

'One careless gesture . . .'

'I don't carry matches. I don't carry a gun. Hell – I don't even wear shoes . . . I was only at the heart of things, watching the sun shiver on the water and listening to the leaves breathing. I didn't know a Baptist boy's binoculars were focused on my behind.'

'You charging the Gamekeeper with voyeurism, maam?'

'Hell, no! As far as I'm concerned that jerk's just another rare bird. I was watching the grasshoppers tearing up in the grass. I like to lie, neat as a nut, among the leaves. So still I don't disturb the mice. Squirrels, chipmunks -- I'd never seen those before . . . There's a smell lying close to the earth, an edge to the air, acid, sweet . . . a crystal of barley sugar on the tongue.'

'Is it true,' asked Judge Schuyler, 'that where you come from men and women and even the elderly walk around stark naked?'

'We all wore a little string around our waists to keep the good in and the evil out.'

'Maam?'

'It's a nice notion, don't you think? Wanting to keep the good in and the evil out? The string, why it's just a *symbol*, you know.'

'Don't get philosophical on me, maam,' he warned, 'I've got an ulcer.' He leaned back, tipping his chair, and closed his eyes. Cûcla thought he had gone to sleep. 'How's the wizard?' he asked suddenly.

'Lamprias has found the Key to Life.' She hesitated. 'Don't hang a rap on me, Boss.'

He opened his eyes.

'These are not my laws, maam, but society's laws. One woman starts walking around unclad in a protected environment and pretty soon a colony of kooks are picketing the place, trampling the stinkweed, frying owl's eggs sunnyside, doing their business in the bushes. I used to go fishin',' he confided, 'up to Kinderhook Creek. Nudists moved in there and within three months the fish had all choked to death on French letters.' French letters? What the hell was he talking about? 'It's an imperfect world, sweetheart. I wish I could let you off, but I can't.' He contemplated the bubbles bouncing off the ice-cubes in his freshly filled tumbler. Cûcla was fined fifty dollars for trespassing and one hundred and fifty for exposing herself in public.

It is not easy for me now to look back on all those years in logical order. I remember that once we were invited to a party and Cûcla pulled out an enormous harmonica – the biggest harmonica that I have ever seen – and it was painted bright green. Where in the name of heaven had she learned how to play the harmonica?

'In the kitchen. There's this hobo, Dusty Grimes, from Alabama; he comes by for blueberry pie. He taught me.' A hobo? I thought about it. I had to ask her what a hobo was.

She took up belly dancing. It made her happy to be bumping and grinding with a group of ladies and she brought them all home – some silly, some solemn, some with poor posture, some lovely – and all of them danced. One belly dancer is a lot for one man to handle; Cûcla brought home fifteen.

How does Cûcla find the time? When the Chief Fireman promised to let her beat the drum at the next barbecue, she joined their brass band. But the day I saw them play, Cûcla was first trombone.

Mr Tufts and Cûcla got along famously. He was knocked off balance by a strange ailment he characterized, for vanity's sake, as 'a rare, viral disorder', but which was in fact psychological. There were days, even weeks, when he was unable to utter a single word and communicated with a child's slate and a squeaky piece of canary-yellow chalk.

good day. tea? oolong? sit down. back in a jiffy.

Mr Tufts lived alone in a house riddled with cranberry glass and *millefiori* paperweights he had inherited from his mother, Marguerita, a moon-faced woman with a surfeit of teeth whose photographs cluttered the plaster mantel.

Mr Tufts was a stunted man, yet kind, and droll. He gave Cûcla the books that were to become her greatest friends: *Alice in Wonderland*, *The Snark*, *The Wind in the Willows*, *The Wizard of Oz* and Kafka's *Metamorphoses* which she read to me in bed, stopping again and again to roar with laughter. I found the story downright frightening and told her so. Cûcla insisted that I'd not understood; perhaps I hadn't really been listening. When I said I had and that the story scared me, she called me an old foof. My quivering wand, teased by her toes, proved otherwise.

'Look,' I said, 'see: my staff is as green as your harmonica!' And she, my Katzenjammer Cûcla:

'Wow ZOUKS! Lamb, YOWEE!'

You will understand why later, when Senator McCarthy asked me if my companion was a Marxist, I answered without hesitation, Yes. Of course, I was thinking of Groucho.

Cûcla was curious. What had Marguerita done to her son's voice?

'Mr Tufts' mother,' she said, 'can crack coconuts with her

teeth.' I expressed surprise. I did not know that Mr Tufts' mother was still alive.

'Dead,' Cûcla said. 'Dead as a doorknob but still breaking balls.'

'Say, Mr Tufts,' she asked at last, 'just what *was* Marguerita like? She's got some teeth! Real skull-crushers! She looks, beg my pardon, like a terrible sourpuss.' Mr Tufts made an unpleasant choking sound and stumbled off after his slate.

my mother?

'Yeah.' (Almost at once Cûcla had picked up *yeah, you guys* and *cripes*.) 'Cripes. All these creepy snapshots!'

fastidious person

'Fastidious? How's that?'

always took excellent care of her teeth

'Heck, Mr Tufts, you need an animal in here, something soft and – Hey! You know what? Pentacle's cat had kittens.'

Pentacle lived in a Victorian house that a previous proprietor had painted purple. A dandy, he was said to own seventy-five pairs of shoes and as many hats including porkpies, beaver beanies and King Fouad's own abandoned felt fezes. At home he sported a tarboosh. When Cûcla visited him with Mr Tufts, he was working on his greatest sham:

ANTHROPOPHAGY OF YESTERYEAR AND CONTEMPORARY CANNIBALS
. . . Our ancestors, crouching in sooty caverns, roasted human bones in their fires and split them to extract the succulent marrow. The grizzly remains of these feasts can be found scattered throughout the world; upon the bones' spongeous extremities are discernible the dents, pits and scrapings of human teeth . . . Von Pfeifertits insists that the

teeth marks are not human and that the red ochre dabblings are proof enough these are the remains not of hearths but of funerary pyres. But Von Pfeifertits, with all due respect, has spent his life in the tame corridors of the University. What does he know of real life?

Several times throughout my travels in Blackest Africa, the obsessive penumbra of Deepest Amazonia and the obscure Far Reaches of Tantric Tibet, I have myself been forced to taste human meat. It is therefore with the dolorous certitude of first-hand experience that I write these lines . . .

Lines so typical of HP's inflated style!

Mr Tufts found his happiness in a tiny, tiger-striped cat, mocha and coffee and not yet three months old and who, Pentacle lied, had been brought up solely on human milk. A loner, Tufts had heard nothing of Pentacle's eccentricities: his wife entertained bare-breasted and his girlfriends – all secretaries from Albany – spent their weekends in his living room naked and locked up in cages.

'I am delighted you are taking her,' said Pentacle to Tufts, 'she deserves a good husband.'

'She?'

'Look here!' Swinging the kitten by the scruff of its neck, Pentacle presented its hind-quarters to Tuft's mouth.

'The males have a little hole; the females this charming slit –' He winked lasciviously. Mr Tufts blushed.

'Feed her lox . . .' he continued as they walked back to the car, 'and roast beef. Give her a nice box of fresh sawdust, else she stain your carpets and a log else she scratch your furniture. She has fleas—'

Although that day in voice, Mr Tufts was silent.

Soon after Pentacle showed up with a bottle of Tequila, Cûcla ran into the kitchen for some salted nuts. HP pointed out that apes eat nuts—

'On the other hand, man relishes meat, raw meat, the reckless aromas of roasts. We must look for our ancestors elsewhere. By the way, y'have any cold roast pork around?'

'I was brought up to refer to the apes as "Uncle" and "Aunt",' Cûcla said. 'How about a tunafish sandwich?' Pentacle followed her into the kitchen.

'I've gotta admit, sweetheart,' he said, shifting gears, 'that I came here tonight with a proposal of collaboration on my next book. I have a theory which you can perhaps corroborate. I call it "The Exalted Feast". It is my conviction that flawed, luckless Man – mustard and butter – is seduced by his own inexhaustible possibilities for damnation.'

'Phooey' is what I think Cûcla said.

'I am serious. In Timbuktu I have seen people carved up in public beneath the ferociously glittering eyes of King Buktu's wives—'

'King Buktu of Timbuktu?' Cûcla frowned. She handed him his sandwich, but first she stuck in a paper flag.

'In clay ovens crusted with salt and the grimacing masks of gods whose names I dare not mention, in gold casseroles squeaking with grease, bake and bubble the buttocks of—'

'This guy is *weird*!'

'I was there during a religious holiday and saw within the hour slaves buggered and braised; I have recipes—'

Suddenly Cûcla was furious. Stamping her foot she shouted:

'My people were not cannibals! Can a pinch of white ash in a bowl of banana soup be called anthropophagy? I cannot help you, Mr Pentacle. You will have to write your book yourself.'

He was all at once apologetic.

'It is *I*, sweetness, who is the cannibal! I never dared suggest

. . . How do you think a poor grub like me could otherwise survive? I always did my best to accept graciously what was offered; the Niams, the Maoris, the Moubatos all think it a great joke to eat anthropologists!'

'You're just grand-standing! If I believed you, why heck, I'd ask Lamprias to throw you out!' (O my lioness, how I loved you at that moment!)

'A terrific broad!' he cried, undaunted. 'OK, Cookie, you've got my number. I made it all up or I read it in books. Never been farther East than Hoboken or farther South than Albany, But I tell you, this book's gonna make a fortune and, if you'd consider the idea of a collaboration, I swear we could both be in the gravy. No pun intended.'

'Huh? You've never been to any of those places? You've never even been to Jersey?'

'I have a large number of wives and animals that need looking after—'

'Hermes,' I said, directing him to the door, 'let's not keep your wives and their many animals waiting.'

'I'll be back!' he warned. And for months he sent Cûcla gifts – cases of Florida grapefruit, fancy chocolates in heart-shaped boxes, the complete works of Groddeck – or he dropped by, penitent and shy.

'Kinda sweet. So unhappy, really. He only wants to be interesting, poor humbug that he is. In fact, lamb, Hermes is really a lot like Mr Tufts when you get down to it. All they really need is bucking up.'

Cûcla was forever attempting to save people. Even a lard-dripping like Pentacle should be given a chance.

From time to time Mr Tufts and Cûcla took short trips downriver to the city. Sometimes Pentacle tagged along. These trips took on the appearance of pilgrimages with stops for tea at the Ritz's Japanese garden, a visit to the aquarium where they gazed for hours 'mostly at the squids' and an early dinner of chowder at Fraunces' Tavern. I remember an hysterical phonecall from Mrs Pentacle and assuring her that yes, her husband had gone to a ball game. Back home late Cûcla tumbled into bed with gifts of kumquats and socks embroidered with the words: Yankee Stadium.

They also went to the movies. In March, 1930, Cûcla and Mr Tufts saw *Animal Crackers* six consecutive times. The first time they saw Harpo they fell off their chairs. Mr Tufts had found *his* Doppelgänger.

Cûcla carried a brick with her to the HUAC hearing. 'Ignatz always carries a brick to a rendezvous with Krazy' (her explanation to the press). The brick – taken from her at the door and the very one that Septimus pitched through my window so long ago – was photographed and appeared on the front page of the Dutchess County *Midnight Sun*. The publisher sent her a copy, along with the latest *Pogo*.

Once Cûcla sat on top of a giant lobster at the Oddfellows' convention. At the clambake later on in the evening, she, tipsy on beer, sang *Tit Willow* and, to my amazement, juggled clamshells. The shells looped silently in the dusky air, as softly and silently as bubbles rising in water. She was so graceful she might have been swimming. Or I dreaming.

CHAPTER FOURTEEN

EXEMPLARY CAVALIERS

Septimus de Bergerac

The German army entered Angers on June 19th, 1940. I stood on the sidewalk before the Hôtel de Ville to greet them and checked my watch when I heard the sound of their boots, hundreds of boots, approaching. Three o'clock, a Holy Trinity of hours. Wave upon wave of impeccably outfitted soldiers goose-stepped through the streets towards me, a lesson to all in faultless form, in synchronicity. The sound of their boots was the sound of a paddle striking flesh, only very much louder: THWACK! THWACK! THWACK! THWACK! My heart leapt with excitement when Général Von Boeckman, commander-in-chief of the Armies of the Great Reich, appeared in a shiny black motorcar and skipped up the steps of the Hôtel de Ville. Within seconds the frayed and faded flag of our delusions was replaced by a stunning swastika. My own native city had become the seat of the *Militärverwaltung* for the entire south-west.

M'man graciously opened the house to the SS and, until the summer of '44, we had the pleasure of the company of Obersturmbahnführer Roll and Möpse. Having those spiffy young men did wonders for M'man, ever the Grande Dame but frankly getting on. As her knees were failing her, Möpse took to carrying her upstairs to bed. He had Kindergarten's bounce and physique (Kindergarten had both his feet flattened hailing a Panzer and spent the rest of the war in the hospital – a lamentable accident) and I do believe M'man imagined that Möpse *was* Kindergarten. How else explain the trusting way she offered her poor posterior for frications? Roll and I saw to the warming of her nightcap and, as she sipped her eggnog, tucked between feather bed and bolster, the three of us, Roll, Möpse and I, beamed fondly down upon her. Both men had left ageing mothers behind in Würst.

What splendid times we had! More than once I joined them for dinner with the *Admiral* Doenitz at the Château de Pignerolies. Day and night as the rest of the city lay in frigid obscurity, the house on Monsecret blazed. One day I saw the Führer himself reviewing his troops in the park of the *château*. What a figure of a man he cut, his chest as tight as a barrel, his emphatic nose and trenchant gestures cutting air. In all modesty, the Führer looked a little bit like me!

Ah! Here is the cherished photograph of Roll and Möpse standing beside one of the lions in the Jardin du Mail, there where True Man once took a pony ride while I was forced to sit sulking in a cellar. Roll beams between the lion's legs and Möpse, in riding boots and breeches, his officer's cap tilted rakishly to one side, leans with arm outstretched against the lion's rump. His boots, sporting a high shine, have been polished by a young lady who, picked up after curfew, spent the night in jail up to her neck in officer's footwear.

P'pa, there are fools who wear sackcloth and ashes when they could be cutting sharp figures in Italian silk suits; stubborn sons-of-guns who bellyache after meagre repasts of turnip, when they could, like me, dine like princes among the young wolves of the *Abwehr*, the Führer's right-hand men, the masters of time, space and of the future. I've just eaten baked ham, *foie gras*, a swastika of tomato aspic with Möpse and Abbé Alesch (thanks to the confessional, one of our most precious spies) at home on Monsecret among a brilliant company of robust, valiant men who, like myself, believe with all their hearts in Perpetual Renewal, the ruthless battle for Progress and the regenerating force of the National Socialist Project –

a Project which will, once and for all, pull us from the entrails of darkness and propel us out into the light transformed: Exemplary Cavaliers of Superior Humanity.

We walk in the shadow of Death, it is true. There are those who complain that these days their neighbours are shot down on street corners, against the walls of public buildings, at the edges of ditches; that blood pours out from under doors, that cadavers show up in cinemas, the grocery, in school courtyards, at church. These are only the victims of their own stubborn blindness. Each and every act of resistance is an act against the Vichy government and the Maréchal himself. Each and every act of expiation is justified.

P'pa, I am sick to death of those who blubber that times are hard and daily life a drag on the morale and their threadbare pocket-books! For those who do not resist, for him who is accommodating, life beneath the boot is sweet. To him who says that to collaborate is to grovel, I answer: I greet the boot with reverence. It is the boot which will crush the Princes of Israel once and for all. Where is the shame? I see honour. Only honour.

To those who continue to complain about the presence of the German soldier – that salutary angel of our renaissance – I ask: do you prefer a France overrun by the Semite hordes? As of today a star as wide as a hand, as yellow as the greed for gold, is visible on each and every Israelite's heart. The eloquence of the star's ubiquity should be enough to convince even the most dim-sighted 'democrat'.

I admit to contentment. I like to sit in a café and sip my *crème* without being forced to listen to the vulgar Judeo-bolshevik chatter of Central-European 'intellectuals'.

This war is waged not against France, but against anarchy. It is a war fought in the name of the Four Virtues: political order, social order, economic order, moral order. And when

I stand in the uniform of FIT – brown the colour of the earth and blue the colour of the sky – on the stage of our handsome meeting room on Monsecret and see my fellow collaborators, the élite of my native city, standing as unbending as brooms beneath the fiery swastika of our aspirations, the bladed swastika of our anger, the vaulting swastika of our hope, I cannot refrain from asking:

'– DO YOU WANT TO SAVE FRANCE?'

'– YES! YES! YES!' (The membership of FIT is unanimous.)

'– AND ARE YOU WILLING TO PITILESSLY CHASTIZE ALL THE ENEMIES OF TRUTH?'

'– THE GUN! THE WHIP! THE NOOSE! THE KNIFE!'

'– IS THIS THE END?'

'– IT IS THE END! IT IS THE BEGINNING! THE END IS THE BEGINNING!'

And we sing. We sing, P'pa, of our initiatory itinerary which includes murder. We sing of our need for prisoners of sacrifice. We sing of the blood of impure infants. We sing of our northern origins. Of masculine energy. Of the regenerating power of Truth.

The new man is a column of light shining, shining, P'pa, between terror and ecstasy, between earth and sky. Progress is a shedding of old skin and, if need be, a skinning alive. The triumph of Order is at hand. And each stroke of the sword I wield cuts off a slice of your life, shortening the gangrenous umbilicus that joins us. Revenge is the companion who keeps me from throwing this body you engendered from a bridge; revenge and this chance to see brought to fruition the Master Plan of my childhood fantasies.

Time is on the march and Time is on my side. Like fish and bread I am multiplied; the armies of Hitler, upright and invincible, fan out in all directions like the spokes of a wheel. And France – the France of philosophers, Protestants, dissimulators, atheists, heretics, impostors, the spontaneous, the autonomous and the perverse – lies crushed beneath this wheel.

France is purged; the Victorious Legions are her enema.

This morning we arrested that strumpet, your old cohort Jane, alias The Spider, *L'Amazone*, who, foolish enough to think her fame would protect her harlot's skin, met with a senile Resistant known to us as 'the Dubliner' whom we have been trailing for weeks (and who, curiously, has only one eyebrow). Any number of things are now clear to us. Upon the invitation of a certain Mother Superior of a convent in Toulouse – a convent where Jewish children, taken from their families and supplied with false certificates of baptism, have been placed in Christian homes and orphanages (talk about a basket of crabs) – The Spider had set herself up in Nice as the directress of a theatrical school for gifted children. 'Gifted', my arse! Their only 'gift' was to have been born Jewish! (Need I describe the evil 'gifts' of the witches of Israel, those worshippers of Baal who bend, horned and simpering, over the cribs of such babies? Gifted for insurrection, yes! Gifted for calumny and robbery!)

With the help of 'the Dubliner' – a degenerate, given to drink and philandering with antiquated actresses and who has 'connections' in the port of Marseille with traffickers in flesh and in goods of all kinds – The Spider, using the smoke-screen of 'theatrical performances', succeeded in slipping children – just how many I do not know – into Switzerland via Italy and into North Africa via Marseille. I should add that the noodle-headed Italians, in whose veins tomato-sauce simmers and not blood, are demonstrating unheard of leniency with the Jews and causing the Vichy police and the Gestapo no end of trouble. Jews are slipping into the Italian Zone and through our fingers like filthy water. If The Spider's subterfuge has been so effective, it is only because the macaronis look the other way. I have written numerous letters to Xavier Vallat asking that anti-Jewish measures be rigorously applied in the Italian Zone.

The Spider put up a terrific fight and refused to calm down even when her arms were broken. Strange, but it takes the edge off my anger to tell you this; I hate you less just now, but I relish your pain as I tell you that I kicked her in the knees as Möpse held her by her breasts. The false eyelashes turned out to be real enough and left blood on her face and my fingers; when we dragged her downstairs, she didn't kick. Her effects were burned in the hotel lobby. The management has apologized and promises to scrutinize its clients with greater attentiveness.

The wheel of fortune is turning, its axles greased with the bodies of misfits, mulattoes, Muskovy geese, mutton-heads, matricides, magicians, melancholics.

I will tell you a secret. Something about myself. For admit it, you scoundrel, you know nothing at all about me, nothing about my childhood, its terrors, its fevers!

More than once I caught a glimpse of Mademoiselle Parfait's *whosis*, as she crouched with sloven perversity above the chamberpot and thought I saw a hairy wound and knew that one day you would return to put me beneath the knife as you had done to all the women in the house. After, in that shameful sea, I sometimes saw blood.

O my sleepless nights of vigilance and sortilege, lugubrious and sinister! Chimes and rattles alarmed my brain and visions: I have seen the errors of Napoleon, the flooding of great Babylon and rabbis sucking spermy coins and Jewesses with skirts like greasy bells and leeches feeding at the breasts of

Mother France and even cats! My infancy was labyrinth and atrophy; epilepsy, corruption, contamination and eruption. Strangulation! Famine!

The guillotine is not quick enough and here, once again, the Nazi mind shows its superiority. When all the world is Pandemonium, Plutonian, the oceans a pestilence worse than the summer stench of the trenches of war and the mountains cracked open like the heads of men and the forests reduced to offscourings and ashes – THEN WILL I AND MY MOTHER BE REDEEMED.

My mission I saw clearly, young: to divulge the truth of the Jewish stranglehold of the Motherland and to frighten the cowering half-breeds from their caverns and opulent palaces; to thrust them one and all into the nauseous suffocations of rooms wherein all air has been replaced by gas.

Do you love Jane still? So! You thought I didn't know? P'pa – I know it all. *I know everything.* I am your life's hangman's noose and chair kicked aside. I am the lion gnawing at your hide.

I am the eye you carry in your arse.

Your son who reviles you.

Septimus de Berquac

CHAPTER FIFTEEN

HAPPY BIRTHDAY, MARÉCHAL!

Septimus de Bergerac

In my capacity as president for life of FIT I visited Vichy in March of 1943 to wish Maréchal Pétain a happy birthday. I was accompanied by Monsieur le Curé and three young children who, each dressed in a different colour, blue, brown or red, had prepared a small but lively song for the occasion entitled: *Children of the Future of France*, the words written by myself and the music composed by the priest. The children – chosen for their peerless complexions and proven ability to stand quietly for several hours together – had the chiming voices of their innocence, an innocence reflected in eyes that, as Monsieur le Curé noticed, stirred the bowels; I believe he meant the heart. Lovely as they were, even-tempered and docile in the priest's car, proving themselves circumspect at table during lunch and prompt to bed after supper, the two boys blossomed with the chicken-pox in the middle of the night, and, in the morning, the girl finding herself alone, and like the most belligerent oyster, would not be prized from stubborn silence. I set out in the park and, after several hours, found a pretty seven-year-old with an amenable mother. Beneath the spa's roofed paths she learned to sing with brio:

Children of the Future of France
Words by Septimus de Bergerac

Pious souls and optimists unite!
Universal conscience will be proven right!
We have unmasked the clever minions of Satan:
Jews, Anglo-Americans, Russians and Free-Masons.

Small-fry though I may be,
I am a loyal soldier.

Tra la la!
La deri dera!

And making a shy curtsy, Angéline (for that was her name) proved that she could also lisp with guileless charm:

'And long life to you! And best returns of the day! O Maréchal: Septimus de Bergerac and the loyal members of Friends In Truth, wish you a very happy birthday!'

At five o'clock, in time for tea, and while Monsieur le Curé bathed the feverish brows and nasty pouts of the other three, Angéline and I visited the Maréchal in the Hôtel du Parc, room thirty-five. Bloated with pride, Angéline's mother waited for us just outside the door.

Maréchal Pétain was sitting up very straight in a newly upholstered red chair. He was an impressive figure with a great, white head that could have been carved from basalt. He looked Roman, and I recalled that Vichy had often been visited by Roman emperors in the past, men who reclaimed godlike vigour in the spa's salty pools of sulphurous water.

Prodded by me, Angéline began the song and, to my dismay, burst into tears before she was done. But Le Maréchal, who is inordinately fond of children, stood to pat her head and asked us to join him for a cup of cocoa. This was unexpected and I was greatly honoured. A maid brought in a small table for our chocolate, Angéline's and mine; the Maréchal took his at his desk, the top of which was very clean. A large, white napkin embroidered with the double hatchets of Vichy spread over his chest and knees, I saw that like that Jew Proust, whom I need not mention, the Maréchal liked to dunk his *madeleines*. Angéline continued to bawl and would not be comforted, not even when the Maréchal proposed to lift her up into the air

on his cane – a trick he relished with little girls. One look at
the famous cane and Angéline, whom accumulating evidence
was proving to be an inordinately foolish scamp, rent the air
with a shriek. The Maréchal's personal physician came run-
ning from an adjoining room and showed her to the door
where, Heaven be praised, her mother was still waiting.

'*Mon Maréchal*,' I said, once we were alone, our cups of
cocoa freshly refilled, 'my visit to Vichy has been thus far most
instructive. I do not doubt that you realize that a finer example
of the mongrelization of Occidental architecture cannot be
found anywhere in France: Venetian ball-rooms, Tunisian
tea-houses, Russian cottages, the Moorish influences visible in
the casino and the mosaics of the first-class baths. Vichy is
bordello, mosque and hammam – the Muslim Promised Land!'

Coincidentally, Rostand's *Cyrano* was then being per-
formed at the casino and Pétain wanted to know if I was
related to the original. I assured him that I was not.

'So typical of the period, is it not, *mon Maréchal*,' I con-
tinued, 'this taste for exoticism? It got worse in the twenties
– I am thinking of the Negroid Fever that seized the capital,
the so-called "jazz-bands", Yahoo scalp-dances! And the cult
of *L'Art Nègre* which still clings like a scab; do you recall how
one could not go into a museum without seeing the sort of
rubbish sea-dogs used to stuff into their duffel bags! I say:
burn it! Burn it all –'

The Maréchal's eyes were blue. Never before had I seen eyes
so empty of emotion; they were perfectly wonderful eyes, the
eyes of a bird.

He closed them, the better to concentrate; I could tell that
he was hanging on to my every word.

The Maréchal was sleeping. His doctor was delighted;
Pétain suffered from chronic sleeplessness. I stood up to go,
unintentionally awaking him.

'Who are you?' he asked.

'Septimus de Bergerac, Friends In Truth, *mon Maréchal*.' I thought that the time had come for me to tell him all about the various activities of FIT.

'Tremendous quantities of jewellery, bandages, furniture, medicine, toys, shoes, hats, curtains, dishes and so on and so forth have been removed from the homes of deported Angevine Jews and redistributed among needy French families.'

The Maréchal had asked for a pillow which was brought to him; the doctor took his pulse and the Maréchal said:

'To succour the needy is laudable.' I thought that M'man herself could not have said it better.

And so I spoke with Pétain for over an hour during which time he listened with great interest except when he nodded off, which he did twice (not surprising when you consider his age), but never for very long. In admiration I took my leave of my Maréchal only to be at once pestered by Angéline's mother, who insisted she deserved financial retribution for the loan of her brat. Always forthright, I did not mince my words, but told her plainly that her daughter was a bleeding milksop, and that Pétain had done her too great an honour when he had received her.

'Your daughter was given hot cocoa when she deserved a hot thrashing. Should you persist, I will give you both a taste of my cane, seeing how Angéline so rudely refused the Maréchal's!'

It is true that Pétain was known to love children; I myself have never trusted them and my experience at Vichy was proof enough that my distrust is justified.

The visit to Vichy had submerged me in a flood of memories. Shortly after True Man's execution, M'man and I had gone to the mineral springs at Aix where she had been treated for asthma and migraines and I for a rash, shortness of breath and pains that tore into my throat and neck worse than Spain's iron collar of torture. We stayed in the Hôtel Excelsior where we shared a room of pink marble. I was my M'man's escort in the park, the casino and the dining room. I suppose it was very like a honeymoon. We listened to Wagner in the temple of Diana and played pinochle in a room with pillars of lapis lazuli. Everyone there was elegant; if there were any Jews about in this equally, undoubtedly Roman site, they were cleverly disguised.

CHAPTER SIXTEEN

SIDE SHOW

Septimus de Bergerac

Shortly after my visit to Vichy, I conceived an educational exhibition for the benefit of Frenchmen young and old. I even travelled with it and upon several occasions Roll and Möpse joined me. However, it was I who constructed the wax tableaux, executed the stunning illuminations, created the picturesque artifacts.

Among my other accomplishments I have dabbled now and again in oils – and not too unsuccessfully (if a son may trust the unprejudiced consideration of his mother). Roll confiscated a large theatrical truck and several months' supply of gasoline. Once the younger members of FIT had covered its vulgar *commedia dell'arte* masked buffoons with a spanking skin of shining white paint, I – with all the bravura of the consummate calligrapher – painted:

SEPTIMUS DE BERGERAC
*****INSTRUCTIVE*******SCENES*****

and some of the well-loved images of the Jew's perfidiousness: Judas counting coins, Dreyfus stealing secrets, Jesus insulted by the shoemaker, the sacrifice of babes to Baal.

The Museum of Natural History of Paris provided a splendid collection of bottled monsters; these would demonstrate the untold dangers of interracial breeding. What did it matter if some of the foetuses we exhibited were not human? Should an impressionable young person see a two-headed crocodile and take it for a Jezebel's *abortus*, all the better! I can assure you that nothing anyone can say ever after will undo a knot so judiciously tied.

One climbed a ramp to reach the inside of the truck. Within, the visitor was greeted by a striking series of twelve scenes, all of historic and emblematic significance. Here rabbis frankly commerced with the snickering princes of Hell (these devils all had two faces – fore and aft – and aft they coughed up smoke); Simon the Magician rode a chariot of fire, a Jewish thief hung from his neck between two dogs and an infant's head – transformed to teraphim – winked upon the wall. There were names and photographs of Jewish novelists, film-makers and politicians; there were charts as well, and maps of course, pigtails, circumcisions and prophylactics. Each image smacked of Truth; each was more appalling than the next. A meticulous array of plaster casts gave the whole a most palpable credibility. I had sculpted everything of wax, following the dictates of common sense, a not negligible knowledge of anthropology and intuition. A happy *ménage à trois* for the ears and lips and noses were more·real than real and – being all of my own invention – had a convincing aesthetic unity. And, if my exhibit was not the only one of its kind, it was the one that thrilled its public most.

Our tours of the provinces were most effective. Stormed at the entrances to cinemas, saluted at the gates of public libraries, and in the schoolyard mobbed. Parked for lunch in Poitiers our truck was stampeded by thirty housewives who had been waiting for six hours on a bread line and were more than eager to get a look at our extravaganzas.

Man needs entertainment. He needs myth; he needs to dream. You didn't see monkeys and apes queuing up behind our truck!

Days of vivifying, giddy camaraderie. Sleeping in the best rooms of empty hotels, ordering up the oldest bottles, waited on hand and foot by bright-eyed hoteliers and their dizzy wives, joking together over our morning's chicory:

Roll: 'Notice how the Anglo-Americans keep missing target? Blowing the cathedrals of France to kingdom come? Oops! *Sorry* – we thought we were bombing the Luftwaffe's latrines!'
Möpse: 'Didya see the latest fashions in Jewish clothing? All made of solid pine – *le dernier cri*!'

After breakfast we would pull into the schoolyard. The sleepy-eyed squeakers, their ears in need of a polishing (and their bottoms too!), their pinafores smelling of bad food and poor ventilation, their hair stiff with lice-lotion (are these, I marvelled, the inheritors of Marianne, my France?), would stand in rows scratching their crotches, itching for a vitamin cracker, for a drink of water, for a quick scuffle, sucking spitballs. But, when they saw our truck, they pulled themselves together quick enough. The bleeding babies, the razor-fingered rabbis, the bottles of living matter run amok – all shut the little buggers up. They would spend the rest of the day glued to their seats as quiet as death as good as dead.

'Screw a Jew –' (My Pétainist puppet-play inspired poetry!)
'Screw a Jew –'
'Screw a shrew!' (For this a tow-headed tot not quite thirteen was slapped.)
'Don't slap the lad!' I told the mistress. 'What the poem lacks in politeness, it gains in exactness. Come, my boy, tell me. What did you learn today?' (A wink at the mistress; a little nod.)
'W – W – Well. W – Well, s – sir –'
'Now then, sonny. I heard the little poem. You said it properly, without once stuttering. Speak up, son, I like your spunk. What do you have to say?'

'There's a Jew, sir! Hiding in my Mama's cellar!'

'Good fellow! Fine, brave little boy! And where's your Papa, sonny?'

'Died on the Russian front, sir, fighting with the German army.'

'Your Papa can be proud of you, son, and we proud of your Papa. Now tell me, where's that cellar?'

'Just three blocks thattaway —' (he simultaneously points and wipes his nose on his sleeve) '— the house with the green shutters.'

And off rolls Möpse, another job well done. As brats gather snots, so we gathered information. For some of us, spring cleaning is the vocation of a lifetime.

'Theth a Gaullist agitator on my block —' (this towards the day's end gummed by a toothless crone who was especially impressed by King George VI riding horsey on the back of a nearly naked Marianne. The hag was given a bottle of brandy and — Möpse, always the joker — a tube of crimson lipstick.)

'Hemth a primming preth, falth papeth an' a radio—'

We were busy. Joyous and eager. Back in Angers there were galas, fund-raising jubilees. Nothing can stop me when I have the floor, not dragons nor jackals nor rockets' red glare. The room on Monsecret grows as still as a graveyard when I tell how Freud nearly choked in a tureen of cocaine, of Doctor Schweitzer raising Cain with negresses, of Picasso's lapses with stable-boys. And all the while I am spreading the word, what are you up to, P'pa? As the planet palpitates beneath the footfalls of Mars Exterminator, what are you doing? Wading in fountains of milk with your pantlegs rolled up, a stowaway in a bottled boat yearning for the unattainable, that greatest of lies, the lie of Beauty — while She balls cannibals and mutes.

Races are extinguished, families made into lampshades, a Jap city levitates, sucked up and chewed to bits by a thrashing medusa vomiting tar and blue fire while my P'pa broods over seminal seas, his head buried in sand (when it's not between Her legs!). P'pa, *chéri*, if only everyone was like you! My work would be so much easier.

You know, you carry this Invisible Man pose too far. For example, what would it have cost you to show up at the custody trial? It was in the spring of 1907; I was fifteen. All afternoon M'man waited for you, but you never came. Couldn't you have given her that one, small satisfaction? You could have shown at least that much interest in us! Rather than fritter away another day in Mariani's dope den, floating somewhere between earth and sky. P'pa, your absence was the last straw; it broke the camel's back. There we sat surrounded for hours by lowlife; M'man dressed in black taffeta had summoned all her courage to face you one last time.

'Will he bring Her?' she whispered into my burning ear. 'Will the melomaniac dare bring his savage Molochist?' She peered discreetly about the room with the hopes to catch a glimpse of you.

The court convened at two; our case was not the first despite my written request. We had to wait for a Gypsy whose feet smelled of cheese and who had stolen a rabbit. An Arab came after – perhaps, P'pa, your Buttons. He had slipped a marrow into the bottom half of a double-bottomed basket. 'Yeeh! I thought this basket honest basket!' Need I mention the Armenian adulterer who followed the Arab? The Rumanian rapist who followed the Armenian adulterer? The Breton bookmaker who followed the Rumanian rapist? The Hungarian harlot who followed the bookmaker? For hours, P'pa, like hexed peasants following a charmed goose they stumbled forth, reeking of garlic, hair oil and vomit. At last, your lawyer stood and spoke. With delirious insolence he told the assembly that Virginie Grenier de Fourtou de Bergerac was a frigid hypochondriac, hysterical, bulimic and given to fits. Cheeks on fire, I held my ears as, sobbing, my M'man pressed me tightly to her heaving bosom; I hugged those orbs I had not seen for seven years. And then our lawyer took his turn – and turned the tables too!

'. . . Virginie Grenier de Fourtou wants to keep everything, everything – and never to see the brute, the philandering drug addict, the blasphemer ever again. Nor does the child' (I affected the most piteous expression) 'whom he has so heartlessly abandoned. The father has not come to court today. He is, instead, at this very moment, sharing a bath with two lesbian actresses and a psychiatrist.'

'The afflicted,' said the Judge, 'deserve consolation.' The Judge and my M'man were of the same generation.

M'man died shortly after the Allied Invasion. When Möpse told her that freckled red-haired Americans would soon be seen on every street corner distributing Juicy Fruit gum, her heart failed. Virginie de Fourtou de Bergerac's last words were:

Geese oil their feathers; water cannot wet them.

She was a deep woman; I have pondered that phrase over and over again and I am still not absolutely certain that I understand exactly what she meant. Was she saying that Americans are oily (which is true – consider how they eat: popcorn, potato-chips, fried clams, Hershey bars) and that because they had won the war it would be hard, very hard, to sink them in the future?

On August 10th, 1944, I saw the flag flying once again at the Hôtel de Ville. The swastika lay in ashes at the bottom of the stairs. Dressed as a washerwoman, I left Angers at once for Vichy and from there I followed Pétain and his government in exile to Sigmaringen in the Baden-Württemberg where Möpse – who was good at this sort of thing – had made me up some authentic-looking papers. By the end of September, I was on my way to Paraguay. I did not travel alone; any number of Germans and German sympathizers like myself were going there too.

I followed P'pa's footsteps all the way to São José where I hoped to find out some compromising information about him. So that is where I go – to Brazil – a small treasure of Jewish diamonds tucked away in the heel of my shoe.

CHAPTER SEVENTEEN

A CUCKOLD OF HISTORY

Septimus de Bergerac

A Cuckold of History, I flee to South America on a jelly of demons, the prisoner of panic, nausea and claustrophobia. Rumours spread behind me black as treacle. My projects congeal like spilled porridge. I must share my sleeping quarters with two clowns, must listen to their balderdash and bragging about the Jew or two they screwed. What do they know of screwing Jews? Bon Voyage! Wish you were here. Wish I was somewhere else.

Cheated out of my first-class berth I am stuck like a sugar-plum in a cabin the size of a gnome's pocket with a pastry cook from Marseille who abstains from soap and a Picard who makes a point of never brushing his teeth. The Picard pontificates from dawn to dark on History. What does he know of History? History, I tell the bore, is ours. Her posterior scorched beyond repair with a swastika. Wait and see – in the end she'll come crawling back on hands and knees, tongue dragging and tail wagging.

I say History is a wayward wife sorely in need of a flogging. She is a thief with a herring down her blouse, a menstruating ninny, a Sapphic nun, a burlesque queen. She is above all the mother of monsters and broken promises. Ask me about broken promises! My youth rent upon the wheel of her indifference like a chamberpot smashed upon the pavement of the street! History, my expectorating cabin mate, sir, is a whore. She has cuckolded all the world's greatest men and I consider it an honour to share the company of Adam, Caesar, Louis XVI,

Napoleon, Archduke Ferdinand, Jesus Christ and Maréchal Pétain.

Water has never been my element. Give me a hot wind. Give me fire. The songs about the sea and ye olde swimming hole have always made me puke. Give me the tundra. Give me the Erg. A glimpse down the hole of an active volcano.

I hate ships and I hate fish. Fish we eat and when it's meat it's cow's heart stuffed with grass. The *Quilombola* is Portuguese, its crew mountebanks and buffoons, a mixed gaggle of goons from Godknowswhere, each one swarthier, cockier than the one before. These Gypsies howl and bray like a funnyfarm on fire and all night long hammer the decks making sparks. I can't make head or tail of their business – sailors are the sons of Satan. The passengers are all embezzlers, petty employees and fairies; my fellow collaborators riff-raff of the foulest water. Loonies like my cabin mates. One can't speak without spitting into my face and the other drones on and on – recipes for sillabub and punch; a barmy project for embalming cadavers in sugar to keep them indefinitely like candied fruit. And what will you use for the eyes? I ask. Raisins? Will you doll their feet up with frilled paper like drumsticks? On top of it the pansy can't take a joke.

I hate vessels of all kinds. Women (the cunts!) are vessels. Referring to True Man, M'man said: A leaky boat never floats for long. Yet in the tub the pugnosed minx chortled to submerge my destroyers. How I loathed bathtime.

'Look! I am an iceberg!' Making claws, True Man hunches over me.

'Stop! Stop that at once!' I shriek, for the bath is become an arctic sea of sickening proportions. Where has Mademoiselle Parfait gone?

'Watch it!' He prods my aircraft carrier with his toe. 'Hey, Cesspit – your ship's struck ice!' Every time True Man calls me Cesspit I want to choke him to death. But he's too big to tackle; however, I have words:

'Your mother's a Chink! And you're a Chinkpanzee!'

True Man scowls. I can see I've hit him where it hurts. I continue:

'Your mother's a geek and a freak and I've seen her take a leak!'

'Your mother,' says True Man, rising from the soapy water like an angry Oceanus from a cascade of foam, 'has a cunt like a hippopotamus yawning.'

The word is new to me.

'Your mother's bunt –' I begin.

'Cunt! You sissy! A hairy hip, hip hurra-po-ta-mus! A horrible pot of mus—'

His screams bring Mademoiselle Parfait, Dust and my mother from every corner of the house. By the time they reach us, the bath water is scarlet. I have torn a chunk of flesh from my half-brother's neck with my teeth: a wound which will make for a thick, opalescent scar and, in the long run, only add to his confounded sex-appeal. All the same, I have hurt him; for weeks he walks about sullen and sore, his head tilted to one side, the better to show off the chip on his shoulder. True Man is bandaged, Mademoiselle Parfait severely admonished and I punished – I spend the rest of the day wrapped in a wet towel in the foetid female midnight of the fruit-cellar, mulling over those horrible words: a hippopotamus yawning! So mortified I forget for once to be terrified of an opacity I fear throbs with the ectoplasmic ubiquity of that necromancer, Savinien de Cyrano de Bergerac.

To this day, I hold Mademoiselle Parfait responsible for True Man's smutty vocabulary. Had I not myself overheard the foul mutterings and evil curses she mumbled in the haunted corners of the closet and kitchen? She had a weakness for my half-brother and in later years I overheard them kissing in the linen closet.

Mademoiselle Parfait even went so far as to pity Dust; I saw the opium-laced sweetmeats she took to her room at midnight, the chicken neck stewing with ginger at the back of the stove, the blankets she smuggled up the stairs, the care she took with Dust's peculiar laundry. And when Dust's nasty, elfin shoes wore out, it was Mademoiselle Parfait who had new ones made – shoes paid for with coins peculated from the grocery box. If M'man had not suffered the shame of our irregular situation so acutely, I am certain she would have sent Mademoiselle packing. But the thought of bringing a new person into our secret made that noble woman's heart sink.

These were the years when the Amazon had swallowed P'pa whole. Periodically, postcards arrived depicting scenes I imagine he thought would interest growing boys: locomotive trains, sea-ports and mygale spiders. The inconsiderate cad was too tight-fisted to send us each a card but instead addressed them to us both: *my sons*. My sons! As if True Man and I were as alike as two Brussels' sprouts of equal weight and freshness. The postcards smelled of cargo rot and the sweat of Brazilian postmen. True Man valued them. He filched them from the grate and those I tore in two he pasted conscientiously together. He kept them in an empty box of mango paste (the only candy I can't eat and the only sweet P'pa sent us). When I discovered True Man's stash of P'pa's trash I shat into the box and laughed for hours at my little joke's audacity. Unfortunately, it was Mademoiselle Parfait who found the mess, rooting about as she must after bad smells. And so the full impact of the trick was lost on True Man . . . I have never been lucky. Fate has always played her slattern's pranks upon me, whenever she has had the chance. Fate and History – the trickster jinxes of my less than perfect Destiny.

I am rocked like a cranky baby in the reeking carcass of this so-called cargo fleeing France, following your shadow, P'pa (and who knows what I'll find?). I'll tell you what I'll find! A bordello overrun with bats and snakes, a fountain filled with scum, and the obscene paintings you paid for with Virginie's dowry. I will squeeze dry an ancient Chinaman (decidedly you have a weakness for the yellow race!) ready to dig out his grimy souvenirs for anyone who asks. And from the window of a disinfected room, I will watch as the Palace of Revenge burns to the ground, a fire that the press will call both an accident and a blessing. Swarming with vermin, the place was a hazard to public health.

The Chinaman couldn't have asked for a bigger funerary pyre. You see – humiliated, destitute and lame – I can still make my music, Old Fart, gas-chamber music.

CHAPTER EIGHTEEN

FATAL ERRORS

Septimus de Bergerac

Just when I was at the lowest, living like a tramp in a tramp's brothel, I was visited with a stroke of luck (and genius!); it came to me during a night of insomnia (the pain is so bad that I sleep, fitfully, only a few hours in the late morning) that I should sell my teeth – the gold ones, that is – and with the *baksheesh* get a doctor. The black bitch, whose room I shared in these extremes of dire necessity (in fact, her closet, as she kept the room to herself for business), fetched a Jew for the teeth. O the stench of Jewry; the *gefilte* stench of shame! But then – I had the cash; *it* had no smell and the Negress brought the doctor (but first she brought me a new pair of pyjamas to receive him properly: I was, at that point, unable to walk).

The Doctor's name (he looks just like Kindergarten!) is Finkelkraut; I tell him of my admiration for the German Race. A man of disarming modesty he cuts me short. *Hop! La!* Down, up, up down – life is like a see-saw. The radiant Doctor Finkelkraut probes my scrofulous self. My legs are covered with globosities, all more or less corrupt. I pay for my fornications dearly. Hard at first, they soften and then begin to smell. Like money, I joke to the Doctor, they fluctuate. He prescribes belladonna. My toe, violet, smooth and swollen, fusty at root and nail, worries him the most. To say the least, he says: *unsound*. My case is particularly grim. To look at me, I say in jest, you'd think I'd spent my life standing in manure.

He touches the ulcers with iodine, even nitric acid. He wraps my legs in taffeta bandages. I drink iodide of potassium in a syrup of bitter oranges. The toe, he informs me, impervious to all my horsing around, and wielding a cruel blow to my courageous good humour, may have to be removed. However he installs me, that very hour, in his own private clinic. Doctor Finkelkraut has devoted his life to the study and care of syphilis! And now I have my own room, clean sheets, all the little amenities: spotless chamberpot, fresh towels, a substantial blonde nurse and even a desk where – as soon as I am able – I will get back to work on the new book: *Profiteers of Democracy*.

The doctor has prescribed baths in sulphurous water. It is brought to the clinic each day in one-hundred-litre containers; the man who delivers it in a rusty truck is a wall-eyed Indio and shifty but the smell of sulphur is authentic enough.

I begin to think about getting better. For one thing, I am sleeping again for the first time in years. Finkelkraut is doing all he can to get hold of the miracle drug penicillin. He tells me that, as soon as possible, I must go to Pivra, Peru, where the exceedingly dry, hot air and the natural, sulphurous spring water will greatly benefit my health. The gangrenous toe which nearly cost me my life – now neatly removed and healed over – causes me no more discomfort (except in times of heavy rain when I feel a prick beneath the nail that I no longer have).

Doctor Finkelkraut tells me that much of my time in Pivra will be spent lying prostrate beneath steaming mounds of mud administered by native women; when I tell him I can't abide the touch of Indians he, looking down upon me with the most curious expression imaginable, asks how I feel about being administered to by a Jewish Doctor! My reaction is vertiginous outrage; but then I am at once soothed by the man's bountiful laughter. What a *card* this Finkelkraut!

Sometimes I have the sneaking suspicion that P'pa doesn't read my letters. All my adult life I have shed letters the way a leper sheds scales. And has he answered? Never! Not once!

The Years Of Glory are over now, but they will return: the beautiful swastika fits the globe so perfectly and spokes the wheel of the world so well. Name a greater catastrophe than to be chased like a red fox from one's own home and country! Had I hung around, God knows they would have strung me from the nearest tree for all the 'patriots' to see; Hobgoblins! Gaullist riff-raff! Degenerate Hirelings!

Bitter! Bitter! My tongue bristles in my teeth with the taste of bilious rancour. And O! The irony! Traincars full of spiteful letters damning my name! And de Gaulle who thinks that Capital Punishment is too good, too GLORIOUS, I suppose, for hoodlums like me, decides to change the penalty *in absentia* to life imprisonment, should I show up asking.

True Man, my round-skulled rival sibling, lost his head for having kaputed a whore. But what did they do to *Harry Trueman*? The maker of bonfires even I could envy? Nothing!

The female sex is always excited by Public Enemies and Public Hangings. Had I proffered my neck instead of ske-daddling, it is as sure as my name is Septimus de Bergerac that before hanging I could have gotten laid for once *gratis*.

I wonder: who is living in the house on Monsecret among M'man's bibelots and furniture? The furniture she waxed day in and out with all the frenzy of a deeply religious woman who knows that *cleanliness is Godliness*? What repugnant Gaullist frog has made our home into his froggery? Day and night, I hear him drumming, drumming his greasy fingers upon the dining room table, smudged and marred beyond recognition or repair, as he impatients for his dinner, the insufferable Brachiopod. What self-satisfied *derrières* press down upon Virginie Grenier de Fourtou's embroidered settees?

What voracious vole is mouthing M'man's *porcelaines?*
Tonguing her spoons of silver and vermeil? Liberty, my arse!
Democracy, my purse! France is become a holocaust of souks.
All the little froggies, born half-wits, with humps and hooks
or cursed with spastic tics, harelips and hides the colour of
café au lait. Progressives, libertarians, liberals and libertines –
CRIMINAL CRETINS I CALL THEM, DRUGGED
ON THE PIEBALD SUNRISES OF IDEALISM! Look
at the perfect social structures of bees and ants. What do they
know of 'freedom'?

Françaises, Français: soda-pop and bubble-gum, obesity
and acne – that's what your 'liberators' have brought you!

O! The convulsive chicaneries of Fate. A Jew gave me the clap.
Another made off with my teeth. Another with my big toe.
But Tic. Toc! Toc. Tic! I'm still going strong. Why, I'm as
sprite as a gnat and as invisible; no one sees me skulking in
the weeds or even guesses I am here. Capping the climax of
my audacity, I've made for myself a species of leaf-cape,
festooned with vines. You can't see me, P'pa, but I see you,
you old dingle! Bent over your bottles like a baby in a dairy.
Cuckoo! Cuckoo! It's me! Septimus de Bergerac, the Cuckold
of History, is in America. Treading caterpillars and ants, a
horse-fly buzzing persistently about his head. How, you won-
der, did I do it? Hah! Simple, P'pa, as pumpkin pie. Cleverly
I pirated and sold Finkelkraut's medicines to buy myself a
freighter ticket as wide and as yellow as a Jew's cloth star. (If
only it had occurred to me that *The Goddess of Fujiama* was
fatally Japanese!)

The trip to the USA was tedious and trying. This time the
fare was seaweed, jellyfish and the quivering flesh of living
dolphins which was ripped from the trembling carcass like
bark from trees. Rice is not human food; we ate like parakeets

and nowhere on that listing hulk could I find a fork. But every hour brought me closer to you and I smiled to think I was hot on your heels at last.

I stalk you now in the comforting shadow of *her* idiotic hedges. The apess doesn't look her age. I smell hanky-panky: perhaps P'pa *has* discovered the Fountain of Youth. She's as limber as an eel, indefatigable: prunes and mows and rakes like a trooper, kindles fires, chattering all the while to the birds in the trees – a regular St Francis of Ape-isity! I'd crack her little skull if I could – self-satisfied seweress! (If only I had the flair for snares, the eyes to read the fatal writing in the scrapings of her rake!)

I was set up, right here, behind this boxwood pea-hen, with a spy-glass in one hand and a strawberry malted in the other, when the FBI ripped right in to investigate P'pa's promiscuous soups. They didn't find anything (next time I'll plant something) but they got him into a terrible rage, got her screeching like dawn on the Rio Negro.

Senator McCarthy smelled something fishy. His appetite was whetted as I'd hoped; after all, what's more fun than taking a public figure down a peg or two, especially if that figure is a senile 'intellectual'? And yet, I must admit to chafing disappointment. This guy McCarthy – whom I counted on, Goddamnit! – let me down. And the HUAC had nothing of a sacred tribunal.

The hearings started off well enough. They began with a statement by John Edgar Hoover himself who – in answer to my letter concerning P'pa's questionable activities etc. and in thanks for my small gift – had sent a thoughtful note:

. . . I look with interest at your book, *La France des Vampires Juifs*. I do not unfortunately read the French but

142

I assure you the book will receive the due attention it undoubtedly deserves from my staff.

Sincerely etc.
J.E.H.

'. . . Ladies and Gentlemen, honourable members of the committee, Senator McCarthy, it has been brought to the attention of my agency the suspicious attitudes of one Mr Bergerac. His properties was duly investigated and any number of test-tubes seized for close scrutiny. These objects of evident value to Mr Borgeric, were procured by my agents with some difficulty. Despite his great age (Mr Borick will be one hundred and four this year), he is a man of uncanny strength and almost satanic vitality . . . Any number of these objects was smashed and an agent sustained wounds to the lip. Those tubes examined by our experts did contain nothing other than minute particles of plant life, as Mr Bargerec had claimed to be the case.

'Cocaine was not uncovered, however one bottle of a mixture which possibly contains narcotic substances is under inquiry. Mr Borgernick insisted, with language I regret to say here was more than very impolite, that the bottle was a keepsake not intended for personal consumption. Having taken the trouble to taste it myself I can say it has the texture of treacle and tastes rather like cherry tart, custard, pineapple, roast turkey, toffee and hot buttered toast.

'As Mr Dvjorak never actually married his concubine – a female whose origins, as has been pointed out, are peculiar and who was once previously charged for indecent exposure – he cannot be charged with bigamy. However, certain animalies have appeared in his income tax records.

'Because of big quantities of subversive stuffs, such as collections of erotics (all seized by my agency and under the scrutiny thereof), including obscene ceramic-type pottery from Peru, he and his pompadour have been asked to appear before the House Un-American Activities Committee this afternoon.'

Senator McCarthy: Have you, uh, read subversive books for example—
She: (Interrupting him!) Are you a Snark or a Boojum?
Senator McCarthy: Now let's get this straight, here I ask the questions.
She: OK, Boss, I admit to everything. Poop! Poop! I borrowed the motorcar while the owners were at lunch; Ding Dong the witch is dead; sir, I stole the tarts; I threw the brick at Krazy too:

> The method employed I would gladly explain
>   while I have it so clear in my head
> If I had but the time and you had but the brain –

Eeh! What's up, Doc?
The delirious strumpet! And then she made the sound of what I believe I recognized as Woody Woodpecker's laughter. Ten years ago in France she would have been sent packing in a cow-car for Auschwitz for cracks like that! But I am forgetting, this is a 'Democracy', the people get to yap, chew the fat, it's free, 'don't cost a dime'! And this mucker, McCarthy, a mortal vexation, changed tactics, decided to show how *fair* he is, how Goddamn polite with the ladies!
Senator McCarthy: Don't get me wrong, Toots, I like Indians. Everything I know I learned from an Indian named Charlie. Hell, I was born on a lake with an Indian name.
'Toots!' she shouts, 'OK, Buster, you asked for it!' And the old twat scrambles to the seat of her chair (and she is wearing these funny little plastic shoes that look like they are made of solid ruby), clenches her fists and opening wide her bloody

144

mouth lets fly a maelstrom of casters and cans, an ear-splitting Hottentot hullaballoo:

!KÉKÉKÉKÉKÉKÉKÉKÉKÉKÉKÉKÉKÉKÉKÉKÉKÉ
KÉKÉKÉKÉKÉKÉKÉKÉKÉKÉKÉKÉKÉKÉKÉKÉKÉ
KÉKÉKÉKÉKÉKÉKÉKÉKÉKÉKÉKÉKÉKÉKÉKÉKÉ
KÉKÉKÉKÉKÉKÉKÉKÉKÉKÉKÉKÉKÉKÉKÉKÉKÉ!

It took forty-five minutes to calm the place down. Senator McCarthy dismissed the madwoman:

'Someone tell that loony broad to take a nap.' Then he asked P'pa: '. . . And just what the fuck *do* you do?' P'pa's highly technical explanations gave the Senator an uncontrollable fit of the giggles. He let P'pa go, brought the hearings to a close for the day, went out for a couple of cases of beer and he and a shifty looking man named Dick Nixon spent the rest of the afternoon fishing. PEASANT! BUMPKIN! PEDZOUILLE! He never should have left the poultry and poultry egg farm for politics!

Meanwhile I risk my life. This country pullulates with snakes worse than Brazil. And, unlike the forests of France which are all orderly and tame, the woods are a putrid tangle, a jumble of holes and hollows and thorns. I can't take a step without raising clouds of mosquitoes. And I've picked up some repugnant allergy – I'm all over bumps and swellings and boils – a rash that would even impress that damned quack impostor Finkelkraut.

A young FBI agent named Corky has befriended me. He has brought me some lotion; he says it looks like I've been rolling around in something he calls Poison Ivy. He suggests cowboy boots for the snakes and denim pants for the ivy. But why does everything have to be so difficult? The boots, as it turns out, pinch terribly and the damned pants are so tight I can't breathe, or bend over, let alone digest. And I've caught my foreskin in the zipper twice.

Corky takes me to the movies. We go to the Lyceum Theatre in Red Hook to see *The Thing* and *The Day the Earth Stood Still*.

'Corky!' I tell him, 'Corky!' I say, wanting to give the poor lad something of an education, 'the danger isn't from Outer Space but from Russia! It's not the little green men we should be worrying about, but the Reds!'

'Sure, pal,' he says. 'Just sit back and enjoy the movie.'

Corky *believes* in flying saucers and astrology.

'Star shit,' I tell him. 'And furthermore, astrology is a Semite science.'

'Let's just watch the show, Pepsi,' he says, and for a little while I shut up and we do. Finally I whisper,

'For Godsakes, Corky, don't call me that!'

He says he can't pronounce my name. And seeing how he is my only friend, I try not to let it bother me. I go out to take a leak and bring us back some popcorn.

Corky and I get along. The first time he called me 'Pal' I nearly cried. I've been an Influence and an Important Man, and I've known lots of people, including Goebbels and Goering, but I've never had a 'Pal'. And, as I am homeless with just a humble stake-out at the Annandale Hotel (I've been washing dishes and latrines at the college to survive – washing up the dirt of adolescent Commies – well, I've known worse), after *War of the Worlds*, Corky proposes I move in with him to share the big place he's rented in Barrytown – an eyesore, Victorian and purple. It has a tower and cages filled with fancy potted plants and an enormous lawn. Corky thinks it is just the sort of landmark Marts might choose to land on. I hope to Hell they don't.

'Corky,' I say, deeply touched, 'my entire life has been devoted to Truth; Truth alone urged me to set the FBI to trailing my father's arse like the tail of a comet. Favoured from infancy with sublime intuition and the subtle insight of genius I have, since the age of six – when I first accompanied M'man to market – observed my fellow man. Since then one hundred hundred thousand have fallen beneath my scrutiny: their filthy habits, their noses and their lies, their vain attempts at Glory and their Triumphs, too. As I lay beneath a mound of soothing mud somewhere in the armpit of Peru, I came to a conclusion of rare magnificence and clarity. I know, with all my mind, my tripes, my soul, that, before the Universe ends in a whopping conflagration, *the world will be but one vast concentration camp.*

'My body, Corky, is corroded, yes, but my mind is as agile as a cloud, as luminous as a rainbow. I am a great man, Corky, my pal, if only a shadow of my former self. Never, never, never will I forget your generous perspicacity.

'It has been demonstrated scientifically – in fact, I demonstrated it myself in a pamphlet published in '39 – that all minds (Aryan minds, that is) can be purified and transfigured, even yours. You speak of planets and your infatuation with the stars, but do you know, Corky, do you know – that it is MIND AND MIND ALONE that in the shape of electro-magnetic plasma circles the equators of all heavenly bodies in a constant flow; it is MIND we see in the tempestuous eruptions of our Mother Sun; MIND in the ocean's tides and in the sap of trees?'

Corky, on his way to Vassar or Bard College on what he calls a 'drug bust', says,

'Take it easy, Peps.' But I can see that he is moved. When he returns I will tell him about the dangers of Air Travel and the Utility of a Universal Alphabet.

And so Corky and I set up housekeeping and I drop my

147

humiliating job. It almost feels like old times with Roll and Möpse and Mom, and I whistle while I work. I am learning how to bake brownies.

P'pa's life with her is just like an animated cartoon. It stinks with the turds of fawns and elfish farts. There he sits and gloats – as content as I am ulcerous – and, tonight, as I am lonely. I bark my jealous rage beneath the unblinking, yellow eye of the moon. Even Corky thinks I'm cracked; in fact we had a quarrel.

'Hey!' he said. 'Leave the old guy be. There's nothing there, we looked. He just fusses with his tubes and she just sits naked in the artificial rain like she thinks she's a fucking merman. Buncha loonies if ya ask me!' (This added under his breath and I realize with a shock that 'loonies' includes Yours Truly. As the Negress croons: 'Love is just like a faucet, it turrrrns off an' on . . .')

My rash is worse. Last night in a fever, a frenzy of Brobding-nagian itch, I had an insight into the True Possibilities of Astrology, that Arab science I have always loathed, perhaps erroneously. I have been studying Corky's books, or rather, the books the previous owner left behind in boxes in the basement. Pliny speaks of it with respect and it appears that, if it was an invention of Satanic Chaldea, it was transformed and perfected by the Greeks. Caesar and Horace swore by it and wouldn't put their fingers in their ears without first cross-examining the sky.

I have learned to my discomfiture that my planet is Saturn, black, sad, morose and cold; my metal lead, Vapours and Fog; but that my House, Capricorn, is 'The House In The Middle Of The Sky', SMACK IN THE MIDDLE OF THE CE-LESTIAL ORB! *and* the House of DIGNITARIES AND KINGS! (This makes up for the rest and for Capricorn's 'mediocre beauty'.) By the way, Corky believes that the other races come from other planets.

Perhaps there *is* something, after all, to this science of 'a time for this, a time for that'. Up slides Capricorn and Great Men appear with Great Notions of Spring Cleaning. The Master Race squares its shoulders, flexes its muscles, coughs up the yellow phlegm that has been collecting in its lungs and sends it crashing into the Universal Spittoon where it resounds with Historical Significance. Then, it is the turn of the Twins or the Fish: the Aberrant, the Salt Herrings – and the darkling Gum-Poppers, dazzled by their own suicidal perversity and good luck – triumph. But only for a little while. Because Capricorn will be back and the Bull and the Virgin and the Lion!

It is all at once evident to me what must be done. The stars will have to be harnessed or the Earth's orbit fixed, or Fish and Twins banished to the outer reaches of deepest Cosmic Night. Then will the Master Race stand and rule forever an ORDERED WORLD BENEATH A DOMESTI-CATED SKY.

A thought. An equally momentous thought. (The white powder Corky has given me for the itch seems to do wonders for my brain!) I will ask P'pa *to make me over*. To chuck all that pop-eyed spinach and grow my cells instead; plant me in the world's every sterile womb. We could control the market. I've been studying the Mafia's techniques and Corky says the FBI has important Mafia connections. Slowly, slowly, the planet could be mine. There's no hurry . . . Tic Toc, Toc Tic – I've got all my time. Think of all the happy families. The happy sons! A Papa here, a Papa there, everywhere a Papa!

Corky is really very cute. When he's not calling me 'Pepsi', it's 'Mein Kampf'.

Down up, up down. Things have gone from bad to worse. Yesterday as I crouched behind a bush, I breathed some acrid, purple smoke – *She* was wearing those tight Jewish pants and raking leaves and burning something Corky calls 'Poison Oak'. I awoke in the middle of the night, congested, coughing crickets, my eyes glued shut with sand and pus, my lungs like sooty sponges. Corky thinks that the centre of the earth is inhabited; it is the air: it percolates with red-hot dust and throbs with flying ants. *Ubique daemon!* This air must be chewed before it can be swallowed. And I've mislaid my teeth!

I swear it was a plot. All this time I've been spying on her, she's been spying on me. And she's a sorceress, they all are, Indians, Hindoos and Niggers – with strange uncanny powers over fire, smoke and winds. She was singing at the top of her lungs:

> Take me out to the Ball Game,
> Take me out with the crowd,
> Buy me some candy and Crackerjack –
> I don't care if I never get back!
> And we'll root, root, root for the home team,
> If they don't win, it's a shame!
> For it's one, two, three strikes – you're out!
> At the old, Ball Game.

How I burn! I burn and am consumed by thirst. Corky has brought me to the Rhinebeck Hospital where, between the Devil and the deep sea, I lie seething, smothering and deteriorating by the minute.

The doctor, a Ravioli, a noodle named Spaghetti or Spumone, tells Corky I must be operated on at once, a tra he whispers, a tra-la-la—

I've just had the most glorious dream. I was running, as frisky as a lamb, through P'pa's damned scum-cuckoo-spit-snailery, smashing everything in sight with my canes: leaves, blossoms, roots –

O! O! O! SOMETHING PRODIGIOUS IS ABOUT TO HAPPEN! I see upon the air, as in some infernal magic mirror, the Cosmos like a tapestry of Light and Darkness, the heads of angels to the ninth degree, smiling or frowning as the case may be, but all have wings of fire – Bells, a gun, a spinning house – I'm on my way to Oz.

I see a bottle of black glass. Within, P'pa and his whore embracing white as snow.

I see the globe pierced with the bleeding heads of lambs. A ship at sea in tempest. A cherub throwing shells at me or are they hand grenades?

The clouds are gathering, a cyclone approaching, spitting nails and window glass.

The wing of a raven?

My fur hat?

True Man's perfect skull?

Whatever it is, it is getting closer by the second, yes, yes, I see it clearly now: A TRIUMPHAL HEAD OF BLACK BASALT HURLED IN MY DIRECTION but – and this is curious, Corky, curious – it is falling slowly, slowly as li as light as light as a father . . .

CHAPTER NINETEEN

MARTA STRADA

Lamprias de Bergerac

Today a young man came to the door – a fat boy named Corky. I believe I recognized him as the young ruffian who, just a few months ago, made off with my last and treasured bottle of Vin Mariani. Flushed and short of breath, Corky trumpeted astonishing news:

Septimus is dead. He died last night in the Rhinebeck Hospital of an acute inflammation of the throat and lungs. The doctor performed a tracheotomy, but too late; the lungs could no longer function.

Today I saw my son Septimus as a grown man for the first time. His face – a mask of pits and scars – was totally unfamiliar. Immeasurable envy, insatiable anger, have pressed the eyes into haunted hollows; toothless, ravenous, the mouth is twisted in an expression so sour I swear it could blight healthy trees. What had it been to look into that blasted face when the mind gleamed from those lashless eyes, eyes reduced and dulled by constant flame? I looked into the dead face of my son Septimus and I thought I saw the head of Senhor Rosada darkly luminous in its brazier of ignited Kummel.

Septimus had been in America for the past eighteen months, and, oddly enough, it had occurred to me that the recent harassments of the FBI and the HUAC, the Sons of I Shall Return picketing on the front lawn, singing 'Nobody loves Joe but the pee-ee-pul', the phonecalls late at night from the Minute Woman and HATE – all smacked of his mother's methods.

Paddy Toadall-the-Third is newly ensconced in his great granddad's thriving business, with a new baby son, squeaky as a seal, and all the latest techniques in the art of embalming and window-dressing corpses. However, I ask for the body to be incinerated at once.

And now I think of Septimus. I search my mind for memories. Instead of his face, I see a charred place on the library floor. Or clenched fists, the red knuckles of an adolescent, gnawed to the quick, a blurred figure after the trial, when I lost the right ever to see him again.

Before I left, the young Paddy's wife, a sweet-faced young woman with a wonderfully round, ripe bosom, gave me a small cylinder of silver on a silver chain which, Corky explained, Septimus had a habit of wearing about his neck. This cylinder, of curious manufacture, looks like the sort of étui pilgrims once used to keep relics.

On the way home I opened it and discovered a species of journal written in the tiniest handwriting imaginable on thin pieces of worn cigarette paper. Why has Septimus kept it all these years against his skin, against his heart?

I have thought about little else for days. And it comes to me that, perhaps, in Septimus' mind (for Marta mentions both Septimus and myself), we make a peculiar trinity, a family. But this is wildest conjecture. In fact, this eccentricity of my son's, like all the rest, remains a mystery.

And now I must read all his letters, those letters that have collected in shameful drifts – unopened, potent and poisoned – and all intended for me.

Marta Strada

I did not realize at the time of my arrest that I had with me a scented linen handkerchief tucked away at the bottom of my bathrobe pocket. When my robe was taken from me and exchanged for a thin, grey blanket reeking of poverty, I kept this precious thing crushed within my fist.

During the desperately long nights I lay absorbed in the contemplation of the perfume which, with practice, disassociated into isolated fragrances: violet, jasmine, iris, leather and even licorice. And if a flash of lightning leaves luminous fingers dancing for several instants on the retina, these perfumes evoked seraphs that lay poised for flight, in all their shining glory, above the blasted heath of my misfortune. I inhaled and saw open country, smelled leaves, smelled rain and even felt the warmth of an embrace . . . This humble, yet powerful charm was my only hearth and I warmed myself at its fire.

Violet and licorice recall the indigo sheets I had once dyed myself and evoked that startling morning when – so many years ago – Osiris Cahen and I awoke together for the first time and faced one another with lips, faces and fingers stained blue. (We were both so old when they came for us. Why did they not let us die in peace?)

Hunger! The time has come when I would gladly sell my soul for a peach. When I would do anything, to anyone, in any position and with the whole world watching, for something good to eat. I hate myself, obsessed with food, like some rude dog fixing the table for scraps. Throw me a bone and I will scurry off to gum it greedily. You see, I have lost the rest of my teeth in captivity. I am no longer the girl Lamprias loved among the mushrooms, the gay young girl who dyed her sheets to match Osiris Cahen's eyes! But the letters Septimus found were still young, young enough to burn his prying fingers. Perhaps, had Septimus received letters of his own, mine would have burned him less. But what woman writes tender words to a man who climbs into bed waving a whip? A man who in middle age is mad enough to wear a cat on his head? This cat-business I will explain, but first I must settle my differences with dogs.

A dog has 42–44 teeth. His age can be read by the wear on his teeth.

Something puzzling, downright peculiar happened in my neighbourhood in the thirties. The sociable creatures, such as Rita, a yellow bitch the size of a rolled-up sock who guarded the rabbits with a schoolgirl's enthusiasm, and Fifi, another ratter who flipped shamelessly onto her back at the smallest spark of kindness, were replaced by César, a Doberman cub who within six months had metamorphosed into a killer, said to smell a Gypsy at fifty yards; and Prince, who before reaching the age of two had ripped off the chimney-sweep's black face. Of the friendly and familiar dogs, only little Pastis remained and she faded quickly, after giving birth to a piebald brood sired by a Titan whose smoking muzzle, yellow eyes and iron balls each and every one of them inherited. I saw my neighbours swagger as they walked these beasts and swell like dirigibles with a pride rendered inflammable by the press's hot fantasies of that fabulous monster, the Yid Octopus, who suckled the anaemic teats of Mother France and who stank of Kasher fish, International Intrigue, Subversion and Greasy Money. To hear tell it, the dogs' only fleas were the ones they had picked up from Isy Finkelstein the paper-and-rags man. In Château Fleury, I've had plenty of time to think, and I've come to the conclusion that César, Prince and Titan were the Dark Times made flesh; our worst fears about to snap their chains.

I myself have always preferred cats. People who don't know any better imagine that they are self-centred when, actually, it is the cat's autonomy that unnerves them. People don't recognize autonomy – a rare quality in humans – and if they do, they resent it. In other words, a cat is its own boss and won't be toyed with, as if it were a mere mouse.

Kick a dog and he'll slink over to lick you between the toes, rolling his big sad eyes all the while. A beaten dog will eat his master's dung. Kick a cat and you risk your skin. Anyway, there we were, sleeping fitfully, but sleeping nevertheless, while the monsters were sprucing up for the carnival to come: that senile poodle Pétain, the Milice, the Gestapo and the Führer himself – the man who wears a little dog pasted beneath his nose. Once I was arrested, Septimus asked to have my cat, and had it made into a hat. So that ever after, when he was asked about it (for it was a curious affair, fluffy and spotty – yellow, grey, black and white – Nouche had been a female), he would say, pulling it away from his head and patting it affectionately,

'This was a Jew's cat!'

When I was arrested by the Gestapo in the early spring of '43, I was taken to Château Fleury in a filth-encrusted cattle-car. I don't know where they took Osiris; I suppose I'll never see him again. I shared my misery with one Madame Bazille, whose crime was to have run a lottery from her bicycle, and the Noël Dupoux family circus – sister highwire walkers Annette and Suzette, their brother Popol who played the trumpet and juggled silver-painted turnips, and a chimp named Charles Darwin who was killed and eaten the very night we arrived. A lunatic named Aristide Marquis was arrested accidentally, on his way to the sweetshop to buy a bun. He was sent back to the insane asylum the next day. I heard later that the entire asylum was emptied one night – all the inmates volatilized in thin air.

The blood-spattered truck that took us from the train station to the camp had already collected a dressmaker, a man and his ambulant cinema *The Eye of Buddha,* and six tramps, all very old and who were the first to die of dysentery.

Often people came from the village to look at us. We were horrible to see, stranger than any zoo, our feet and hands black with frostbite and our faces knotted with grief. We begged for anything, anything at all: a scrap of food, of wood, a scarf, a cigarette. We had burned our wooden shoes for warmth and the filthy, tattered blankets we wore did little to conceal our sores and our sore skeletons. We were enraged by lice and hunger.

In the summer, a child who had brought us eggs was severely beaten. She had come to see us like a vision of grace in the early evening. The egg she tossed to me exploded in my hands and I put everything into my swollen mouth – yolk and white, smashed shell – sweetness like a hive crumbling on my tongue. In the fall, a boy who threw a package of cigarettes over the fence was shot down.

Today sixteen of us are being transported to Orianburg-Sachsenhausen via Paris. The children, all of them Gypsies, have made up a little song which they sing over and over:

> Have pity, pretty lady,
> Have pity, Monsieur, Dame –
> We are dying, M'dame.

And so we are prodded, ashen, naked and creaking, into the maw of Death. I still clutch a bit of perfumed linen and, oddly enough, its last message – faint now, above all of iris, yet masked by the smell of nightmare – is of Lamprias de Bergerac who, innocent of his son's future crimes, seduced me with stories of the sexual lives of the flowers on a night dizzy with crickets and blazing, blazing with fireflies.

CHAPTER TWENTY

A LETTER FROM SEPTIMUS

Manaus, undated

TRIBAL PRINCES AND TRAINED OWLS – THESE ARE
THE PROFITEERS OF DEMOCRACY. The world has not
yet been vaccinated: Hate's cleansing virus still flickers like a
thousand candles in the air.

P'pa, mark my words – I'll have the last laugh. And all
FIT's faces beaming up at me once more. Their hunger, one
abysmal mouth sucking up my anger's bituminous lake down
to the last, bitter particle of gall.

It will please you, you adulterer, I'm broke, threadbare, an
exiled hobo and sicker than a dog. Frankly, I could do with a
letter. Why is it you have never written? I am, after all, your
own flesh and blood. And I could use some cash.

To tell the truth, I would do anything for one little sign, one
snot of your esteem. Take me seriously for once! Take my
scabs, take my prick! Take my time, Tic, Toc, Toc Tic! Take
my accursed soul. The flaring heaps of my sleepless nights.
Take my life's savings. (I have none!) Take my temperature,
will you?

P'pa, you fill my mind like some fantastic tumour, a red-hot
squid with spokes. This is my skin, P'pa. I am skinned alive.
Each and every letter a tattoo.

How old *are* you, you decrepit son-of-a-bitch? Six million
Jews have kicked the bucket, flushed away like so much
excrement, and why not you? What are you waiting for? What
makes you so tenacious, you make me sick, you leech, hanging
onto life as if it were a hook!

Still tinkering with your filthy experiments, you sorcerer?

Still living with an ape? One of these days I'll show up just when you least expect me. Last time I smashed your spectacles – do you remember?

Your son,